TAUGHT BY GOD:

An Introduction to Orthodox Theology

TAUGHT BY GOD

An Introduction to Orthodox Theology

HARRY BOOSALIS

ST. TIKHON'S SEMINARY PRESS
SOUTH CANAAN, PENNSYLVANIA 18459
2010

TAUGHT BY GOD:
An Introduction to Orthodox Theology

Copyright © 2010 by Harry M. Boosalis.
All rights reserved.

The icon on the front cover of St. John the Theologian and his disciple St. Prochorus is a detail from an 11th century manuscript of the Holy Monastery of Koutloumousiou, Mount Athos, used with kind permission.

Cover design by Joel Wilson.

Published by:
St. Tikhon's Seminary Press
P.O. BOX B
South Canaan, Pennsylvania 18459
USA

Printed in the United States of America

ISBN 978-1-878997-87-6

For my students

past, present and future

TABLE OF CONTENTS

INTRODUCTION 13

CHAPTER ONE – Orthodox Theology:
2000 Years of Apostolic Tradition

Introductory Remarks 15
Theology as a Sacred Service of the Church 17
The Patristic Way 19
Scholars and Theologians 21
Follow the Fathers 24
The Seminary as a Worshipping Community 26

CHAPTER TWO – Orthodox Theology:
A Way of Life

Theology as a Spiritual Process 29
Theology as Prayer and Purification 32
Theology as Repentance 37
Theology as Charismatic Experience 42
Theology as Participation in Divine Life 44

CHAPTER THREE – ORTHODOX DOGMA: AN EASTERN APPROACH TO THE STUDY OF DOGMATIC THEOLOGY

Preliminary Definitions..49
The Soteriological Concern...57
Dogmas as Definitions..59
The Danger of Systematization..................................67
The Need for a Creed..74
Dogmas Do Not Develop...82
The Mind of the Fathers...85
The Proper Balance...94
Concluding Remarks...96

CHAPTER FOUR – THE ORTHODOX ICON: THEOLOGY INCARNATE

Preliminary Remarks..99
The Theology of the Icon: An Introduction..............100
Icon as Image..103
Terminology: Iconophile and Iconoclast....................109
Iconoclasm: A Brief Overview – Phase One.............110
The Distinction between Worship and Veneration......115
Iconoclasm: A Brief Overview – Phase Two............118
Icon and Incarnation...120
Conclusion...125

EPILOGUE..129

BIBLIOGRAPHY..133

ABOUT THE AUTHOR

Dr. Harry M. Boosalis, Th. D., a native of Minneapolis, received his Bachelor of Arts degree in Philosophy and Classics from the University of Minnesota. Graduating from Holy Cross Greek Orthodox School of Theology (Master of Divinity degree, Class of 1985) he went on to receive his doctoral degree in Orthodox Theology from the University of Thessaloniki under the direction of Prof. Georgios Mantzaridis. He teaches Dogmatic Theology at St. Tikhon's Orthodox Seminary. His other books include *Knowledge of God, Orthodox Spiritual Life* and *The Joy of the Holy*.

All Scriptural quotations are taken from the
New King James Version, unless otherwise noted.

It is written in the prophets,
"And they shall all be taught by God."

The Gospel of John

INTRODUCTION

Taught by God is comprised of preliminary lectures in Orthodox theology. Although intended for first-year Master of Divinity students at St. Tikhon's Seminary, its introductory level of approach makes it suitable for non-specialists as well.

Written in a reader-friendly style with a deliberate attempt at presenting the spiritual themes of Orthodox theology in a clear and coherent way, this book will benefit anyone, regardless of background, interested in introducing himself to the study of Orthodox theology and Eastern Christian spirituality.

Based on Holy Scripture and patristic teaching, this study refers to the writings of a wide variety of Orthodox theologians, primarily those of Eastern European backgrounds. These include theologians from modern Greece as well as the more familiar and well-known writers of the Russian émigré community who first promoted the study of Orthodox theology in the West.

Drawing from such diverse sources, this book is also original in that it is written for seminarians preparing for ordained ministry as parish priests. It preserves its teaching purpose by maintaining a practical approach as well as an appropriate level of language.

Taught by God is ideal for any layman who seeks to introduce himself to, or increase his knowledge of, the patristic approach to Eastern Orthodox theology and ancient Christian spirituality.

Chapter One

ORTHODOX THEOLOGY: 2000 YEARS OF APOSTOLIC TRADITION

Introductory Remarks

The first lesson learned in Orthodox theology is that the study of theology must not be approached purely as an academic endeavor. The study of theology is primarily a spiritual process. The believer must first be exposed to, edified by and ultimately identify with the time-honored Tradition of the Church Fathers.

The Fathers offer a rich inheritance of spiritual tradition established by Christ Himself and passed on from the earliest days of the apostolic Church. Tradition is not confined to the annals of archaeology. Ultimately, Holy Tradition is spiritual *experience*; it is personal participation in the life of divine grace. It is this two-thousand-year spiritual tradition that the believer participates in, and comes to call his own.

By participating in Holy Tradition through his life in the Church, he shares it with those around him. He thus preserves Tradition and passes it on to the next generation. The word for tradition in the original Greek is παράδοσις, which implies a handing over, transmission or handing down.[1]

The student of Orthodox theology must become conscious of his calling to serve as a living link in this two-thousand-year tradition. He is called not simply to *study* Orthodox theology; he is called to *live* it through his own personal experience of participation in the ascetic and sacramental life of the Church.

In the words of the late Elder Sophrony of Essex, "God can touch the spirit of man and give him, directly and immediately, knowledge of Himself. There is a great difference between this knowledge and that which is acquired in theological schools. It can be very dangerous to do theology without having an existential experience of life in the spirit of Christ."[2]

The student must begin to experience Orthodox theology and ideally he comes to personify it in his own daily life and in his dealings with other people. In this light, Orthodox theology is a personal encounter. It is a personal encounter with the personal God and with other human persons. It can be said that theology is also an encounter with one's *true* self, with one's own authentic person as a communal being.

---

[1] See *A Patristic Greek Lexicon*, ed. G. W. H. Lampe, Oxford, 1982, p. 1014.

[2] Archim. Sophrony, *Words of Life*, trans. Sr. Magdalen, Essex, 1996, pp. 34-35.

In this context, the theological experience of our Church Fathers is seen in its proper perspective. It is a living relationship with the same Person whose face the Apostles saw with their own eyes and whose voice they heard with their own ears.[3]

Theology as a Sacred Service of the Church

The student of Orthodox theology must be constantly aware of the fact that theology is a sacred service of the Church to which it is intrinsically bound: "Orthodox theology is purely a service which accomplishes its sacred task *from out* of the Orthodox Church, *for* the Orthodox Church, and *in* the Orthodox Church for the glory of God."[4]

Theology is a way of understanding and expressing the Church's unique experience of the life in Christ. Through her theology, the Church formulates the various aspects of her faith and life, and she presents them to her faithful and defends them against false teachings.

Without this sense of 'sacred service', theology can become simply a science, much like a secular science, with little or no regard for upholding the integrity of the content of the faith. Without this sense of 'sacred service', the student of theology can become indifferent to his awesome responsibility before God, His Holy Church and to those who will be touched by his work:

---

[3] Cf. 1 John 1. 1-3.
[4] J. N. Karmiris, 'Contemporary Orthodox Theology and its Task', *SVTQ*, 13. 1-2, 1969, p. 12 [emphasis mine].

"The theologian must speak to living beings, address himself to living hearts, he must be full of attention and love, conscious of his immediate responsibility for the soul of his brother, and particularly for the soul that is still in the dark."[5]

The questions arise: How to make a faith of the first century more relevant for the world of the twenty-first century? How to uphold and defend the apostolic life in Christ in the face of various modern theological trends of our day? How does the Church, with such deep roots in the ancient world, interpret her life to modern man in the new millennium, where secular Christianity and religious syncretism exert a far-reaching influence that often affects even her own members? Does she simply ignore the vast changes prevalent in the teachings, practices and ethical values of many contemporary western Christian confessions, or does she try to respond and reach out to the world around her; and, if so, how?

---

[5] G. Florovsky, *Aspects of Church History*, Vaduz, 1987, p. 207.

The Patristic Way

In order to meet these challenges the student must not only live a life centered within the liturgical life of the Church; he must also be trained and practiced in the ways of patristic theology. He comes to share, to whatever degree possible, in the same methodology, the same categories of thought and the same manner of reasoning and sound judgment applied by his Church Fathers before him who addressed the contemporary concerns of their own day.[6]

This is how he is able to confront and respond to the needs and issues of his day. He must also be familiar with the currently accepted methods of academic research, scholarly study and philosophical language in order to determine the extent of their usefulness and to facilitate his witness to those around him.

This is the way the Fathers reacted to the various heresies that have confronted the Church. From the gnostic movements of the second century to the heretical teachings concerning the Holy Trinity of the fourth century; to the great Christological heresies of the fifth, sixth and seventh centuries; to the iconoclasm of the eighth and ninth centuries and the hesychastic controversy of the fourteenth century—the Fathers have always responded to their opponents in the language of their day and in contemporary terms which their audience could understand.

---

[6] Refer to Karmiris, ibid., p. 19.

The Fathers were aware of the philosophical background underlying the mindset of the world they lived in and the logic that fueled heresy. They were armed not only with the grace of the Holy Spirit acquired through lives of purity and prayer, but also with the weapons of clear and coherent thought, the persuasiveness of rational argument and the ability of sound reason: "When one lives a holy and sinless life, intellectual knowledge can prove wonderfully fruitful."[7] The formulation of the apostolic teaching into Church dogma demanded both a spiritual as well as a systematic effort on the part of the Fathers.

This same spiritual effort is demanded of students today, as they must first *experience* Orthodox theology within the life of the Church, and only then attempt to expound, express and interpret it in the twenty-first century.

---

[7] Archim. Sophrony, *Words of Life*, p. 35.

Scholars and Theologians

Here we must note a distinction between the terms scholar and theologian. A scholar engaged in the study of theology may not be a theologian in the patristic sense of the word.

From the Orthodox perspective, a theologian is one who experiences God—one who *knows* God and not only knows *about* God: "Theological science, which is taught in schools and has become an intellectual specialization open to all, does not give knowledge of God. Knowledge of God comes from life in God, which is born in the deepest place of the heart. ... One can be a great scholar, with academic qualifications, and yet remain completely ignorant about the path of salvation."[8]

While not limiting the term theologian to a strict and narrow sense, it is still useful to recall Evagrius Ponticus and his classic definition of a theologian: "If you are a theologian, you will pray truly. And if you pray truly, you are a theologian."[9]

It is also worth pointing out that the Church has granted the title of Theologian to only three Saints—St. John the Evangelist and Theologian, St. Gregory the Theologian (Archbishop of Constantinople) and St. Symeon the New Theologian.

---

[8] Archim. Sophrony, *Words of Life*, p. 35.
[9] Evagrius, *Chapters on Prayer* 60, trans. J. E. Bamberger, Kalamazoo, 1981, p. 65; PG 79, 1180B.

On the other hand, no one would deny that there are a great many other Fathers and Saints who also fit the description of Evagrius, as well as countless other theologians throughout the two-thousand-year history of the Church, up to and including our own day.

The point is that the term theologian is often used much too loosely today. Many times it refers to anyone engaged in the pursuit of academic research that happens to have theology as its subject, much like the scientific investigation of any other intellectual discipline. A theologian in this academic sense is primarily motivated by scientific research. He may live his life outside of the Faith, remain indifferent to the personal demands made by the study of Orthodox theology, and have little regard for his responsibility to the Church and to those who may be influenced by his work:

> According to the understanding of the Church Fathers ... it is not possible for someone outside the communion of saints to perceive clearly the teachings of Scripture, the Ecumenical Councils, or in general the Church. ... theology is not seen as consisting simply of penetrating scholarly research. [This] of course is not excluded ... However, the point is that ... scholars of Scripture and theology will not necessarily have the knowledge concerning revelation, the Incarnation, grace and salvation that the saints have.[10]

---

[10] J. Chryssavgis, *The Way of the Fathers*, Thessaloniki, 1998, p. 83.

A theologian in the patristic sense, on the other hand, is one who knows God through the experience of divine grace and whose spiritual life is centered in the ascetic, sacramental and liturgical life of the Church. This is why his knowledge of God coincides perfectly with the teachings of the Fathers. They share the same experience.

Elder Paisius of Mount Athos provides a contemporary example. He writes, "Theology that is taught as a [worldly] science usually examines things historically and consequently understands things externally. Because patristic asceticism and inner *experience* are absent, this theology is full of doubts and questions. With his mind man is not able to comprehend the divine energies unless he first struggles ascetically to *live* these energies, so that the grace of God might work within him."[11]

If we too strive to emulate the lives of our Fathers, to whatever degree we are able, then perhaps we too may begin to be granted glimpses, if even momentarily, into their shared experience and knowledge of God.

---

[11] Elder Paisius, *Precious Vessels of the Holy Spirit*, trans. H. Middleton, Thessaloniki, 2004, p. 141 [emphasis mine].

Follow the Fathers

The primary goal of the student of Orthodox theology today is to uphold the integrity and values of the Church's life and teaching. He is conscious of his calling and his responsibility to uphold the tradition of his Fathers before him. He is always aware of the fact that his work is a sacred service to the Church and that it indeed will affect the spiritual lives of other people.

As the Church confronts the various theological issues arising with the dawn of the new millennium which may challenge her teachings and Tradition, the students of today will be called upon tomorrow to provide an Orthodox response.

To accomplish this task entails not only following the Fathers in their use of theological argument; it requires following their way of life. It means pursuing their same path of repentance, their same path of purification from passions and their same path devoted to prayer. It means participating in their same spiritual experience: "Orthodoxy must encounter the West creatively and spiritually ... Orthodox theology is summoned to answer Western questions from the depths of the unbroken Orthodox experience and to confront the movements of Western thought with the unchanged truth of patristic Orthodoxy."[12]

This is what sets Orthodox students apart from those who are motivated by more philosophical interests. This is what set the Church Fathers apart from the heretical teachers who opposed them.

---

[12] G. Florovsky, *Aspects of Church History*, pp. 181-182.

The way of the Fathers is not some abstract and unattainable ideal. It is open to all who strive to live the life in Christ within His Holy Church. The only thing required is a firm resolve to pursue it. In the words of Elder Sophrony:

> There are two ways for theology: the one, widely familiar in previous centuries, appertaining to the professional theologian; the other, which means being crucified with Christ, knowing Him in the secret places of the heart. The first of these types is accessible to the majority of the intellectually endowed having a preference for philosophical subjects—genuine belief in the Divinity of Christ expressing itself in a life lived according to the spirit of His commandments is not needed. The second is the theology of the confessors, which is born of a profound fear of God in the fiery flames of repentance ...[13]

---

[13] Archim. Sophrony, *On Prayer*, trans. Rosemary Edmonds, Essex, 1996, p. 62.

The Seminary as a Worshipping Community

The seminary experience is not limited to academic pursuits. It is an invitation to live a life of prayer. The patristic path of repentance is made possible through a Christ-centered life anchored within the life of the Church. This is precisely what is at the foundation of the seminary experience.

An Orthodox seminary is first and foremost a worshipping community committed to the life in Christ—a community centered in and around the life of the Church. With all its positive aspects, as well as its spiritual challenges—and there are many—the seminary affords the student the opportunity to strive to acquire, as far as he is able, the virtues of humility and obedience that are required to share in the same ecclesial experience of his Fathers. This shared experience is remarkable for its unanimity and unique continuity stretching two thousand years across space and time.

By sharing the same ecclesial life as their Fathers before them and emulating their same spiritual virtues, partaking in the same sacraments, attending the same services, following the same liturgical cycles, singing the same hymns, reciting the same prayers and following the same ways of prayer, being inspired by the same Scriptural readings, observing the same fasts, celebrating the same feasts, commemorating the same Saints, venerating the same holy relics, kissing the same icons, obeying the same canons, upholding the same ethics, preserving the same practices, identifying with the same theological teachings—and above all, receiving the same Holy Body and Blood of Christ—

all students of Orthodox theology, from throughout the centuries of the Church's existence, share a common Faith and communal experience and are thus united in the timeless and eternal bond of two thousand years of Holy Tradition.

This is the only way that the Orthodox theological student of today will preserve and proclaim the Faith of his Fathers tomorrow. This is how he will keep the patristic way of theology free from non-Orthodox influences that will try to steal into his inheritance. This is how the Orthodox student of the twenty-first century will preserve intact the apostolic teachings bequeathed to him from earlier centuries. This is how he will be enlightened, enriched and inspired as he struggles to meet the demands of his day—through a life in pursuit of prayer, flowing from the font of Holy Tradition.

In the words of the Apostle Paul, "Therefore, brethren, stand fast and hold the traditions which you were taught, whether by word or our epistle."[14]

---

[14] 2 Thess. 2. 15.

Chapter Two

ORTHODOX THEOLOGY: A WAY OF LIFE

Theology as a Spiritual Process

Before one begins to study Orthodox theology, the first questions that the believer must ask himself in all honesty are: "Why am I doing this? Just what *is* theology? What exactly am I getting myself into?"

What is theology? Orthodox theology is primarily a spiritual process. And by 'process' we mean "a *continuous* action or series of events ... *method* of action ... leading to the accomplishment of some result."[15]

More specifically, Orthodox theology is a *personal* process aimed at progress in *prayer*, which is acquired through one's participation in the ascetical, sacramental and liturgical life of the Church.

---

[15] *The Oxford English Dictionary*, vol. 2, Oxford, 1971, p. 2311.

One should not approach the study of Orthodox theology as he would the study of biology, literature or law. Such disciplines are purely academic endeavors. Their main concern is to study the subject at hand using the commonly accepted methods of academic scholarship for intellectual knowledge, usually centered on one specific and isolated discipline. There is little or no concern for the personal growth and spiritual values of the student involved. The acquisition of knowledge is seen as an intellectual process. It has little to do with one's spiritual formation as a human person. The student is preoccupied mainly with exercising the faculties of his 'head' rather than those of his 'heart'.[16]

The same may hold true in regard to theology if it is treated as an academic science:

> Age-old experience of academic theology has shown convincingly that it is possible to acquire wide erudition in the science of theology without having a lively faith—that is, in a condition of total ignorance of God. In such cases theology becomes an intellectual profession, like jurisprudence which differs in each country in the same way as theology differs in the

---

[16] In Orthodox tradition, the 'heart' is seen as the "spiritual center of man's being" and not simply as the seat of the emotions, sentimental feelings and affections; refer to the glossary in *The Philokalia*, vol. 1, London, 1979, pp. 361-362. The term 'head' in this instance refers to the rational and intellectual abilities of the mind.

multitude of confessions divided among themselves.[17]

This is also a potential danger with Orthodox theology. While the student is indeed trained in the ways and methodology of theological research, writing and scholarship, still the study of theology must not be undertaken purely as an academic endeavor, nor become merely an intellectual process. Rather, the head and the heart must work together:

> We tend to separate the mind from the heart. We like to fill the mind; yet, we forget the heart. Or else, we fill the heart with information that should fill the mind. Nevertheless, the two work differently: the mind learns; the heart knows. The mind is educated; the heart believes. The mind is intellectual, speculative; it reads and speaks. The heart is intuitive, mystical; it grows in silence. The two should be held together; and they should be brought together in the presence of God.[18]

First and foremost, the focus must be on the formation of the student's spiritual orientation and the development of his prayer life. Genuine Orthodox theology can never be separated from the student's life of prayer,

---

[17] Archim. Sophrony, *We Shall See Him as He Is*, trans. R. Edmonds, Essex, 1988, p. 204.
[18] J. Chryssavgis, *In the Heart of the Desert*, Bloomington, 2003, pp. 76-77.

since it engages not only his mind, but also his heart and ultimately his whole person.

Thus the student must begin first with his heart and then with his head: "Academic theology is not enough for salvation. Read especially the ascetic Fathers. From them you will learn true theology, the right attitude of the mind and heart where God is concerned."[19]

However, it must be stated, that it is not a matter of simply reading the ascetic Fathers. More importantly, we must apply their counsels within our daily lives. We must follow their example. According to Elder Paisius, "The goal of reading is the *application*, in our lives, of what we read ... If one studies a great deal in order to acquire knowledge and to teach others, without living the things he teaches, he does no more than fill his head with hot air."[20]

Theology as Prayer and Purification

Again, we must ask ourselves, what *is* theology? For the Fathers of the Church, theology is an existential experience of the life in Christ. Theology is the process of the transfiguration of the human person. Theology is a life of prayer and asceticism centered within the liturgical life of the Church and immersed in Holy Scripture. These are means which attract the grace of the Holy Spirit.

---

[19] Archim. Sophrony, *Words of Life*, p. 34.
[20] Elder Paisius, *Precious Vessels of the Holy Spirit*, p. 135 [emphasis mine].

The life of prayer cannot be learned simply by reading books on prayer. It demands much spiritual effort, trials, temptations, suffering, humility and obedience. One learns to pray only by praying. In the words of St. John Climacus: "You cannot discover from the teaching of others the beauty of prayer. Prayer has its own special teacher in God. ... He grants the prayer of him who prays."[21]

Moreover, one does not *become* Orthodox just by reading books on Orthodoxy. Nor does one become a student of theology simply by reading books on theology: "Pure prayer is not given to those who study a lot. In that sense, the path of academic theology is hardly effective, and can rarely lead to pure prayer. True theology is the state of the spirit influenced by the action of divine grace. That is what constitutes the difference between theology and philosophy, between real theology and intellectual, academic theology."[22]

The student of theology must therefore work on himself and on his own spiritual formation. And he begins by commencing a life-long introspection into the depths of his own heart. This necessarily entails an intense spiritual struggle, and the painful process of purification of his passions—and always under the guidance and prayerful support of his spiritual father.

---

[21] St. John Climacus, *The Ladder of Divine Ascent* 28, trans. C. Luibheid and N. Russell, New York, 1982, p. 281; PG 88, 1140C.
[22] Archim. Sophrony, *Words of Life*, p. 34.

St. Gregory the Theologian writes, "Discussion of theology is not for everyone, I tell you, not for everyone ... It is not for all people, but only for those who have been tested and ... have undergone, or at the very least are undergoing, purification of body and soul."[23]

St. John Climacus teaches, "It is risky to swim in one's clothes. A slave of passion should not dabble in theology."[24] St. Symeon the New Theologian also refers to the need for actual *experience* before setting out to study theology:

> You ... who have not arrived yourselves at the perception and knowledge and experience of divine illumination and contemplation, how can you talk or write at all about such things without shuddering? For if we are obliged to render an account for every idle word, how much the more shall we not be tried and convicted as vain babblers when our words touch on such matters as these. For vain babble is not, as some might suppose, just unedifying talk. It also applies to talk ... unsupported by

---

[23] St. Gregory the Theologian, *The First Theological Oration* 3 [*Oration* 27]; trans. F. Williams, Crestwood, 2002, pp. 26-27; *Sources Chrétiennes*, vol. 250, ed. P. Gallay, Paris, 1978, p. 76.

[24] St. John Climacus, *The Ladder of Divine Ascent* 27, p. 262; PG 88, 1097C. Cf. Abba Poemen, "Instructing one's neighbor is for the man who is whole and without passions; for what is the use of building the house of another, while destroying one's own?" *The Sayings of the Desert Fathers*, Poemen 127, trans. B. Ward, Kalamazoo, 1975, p. 184.

practice and the knowledge won from experience.[25]

We also recall Abba Poemen, from the *Sayings of the Desert Fathers*, who was asked, 'What is a hypocrite'? He replied, "A hypocrite is he who teaches his neighbor something he makes no effort to do himself."[26]

Does this mean that one must *not* attempt to study theology until he has actually experienced purification and divine illumination? The Fathers would answer 'no', provided however that the student continues in his attempt to progress and puts his trust in those who have had the experience and accepts their teachings rather than his own ideas and opinions.

For example, St. Gregory Palamas writes:

> As for the man who seeks knowledge before works [i.e., experience], if he trusts in those who have had the experience, he obtains a certain image of the truth. But if he tries to conceive of it by himself, he finds himself deprived even of the image of truth. He then puffs himself up with pride as if he had discovered it, and breathes forth his anger against the

---

[25] St. Symeon the New Theologian, *Ethical Discourses* 1. 12, trans. A. Golitzin, *On the Mystical Life*, vol. 1, Crestwood, 1995, p. 79; *Sources Chrétiennes*, vol. 122, ed. J. Darrouzès, Paris, 1966, p. 306.

[26] *The Sayings of the Desert Fathers*, Poemen 117, p. 184.

men of experience as if they were in error. Do not be overcurious, therefore, but follow the men of experience in your works, or at least in your words ...[27]

The student must not be fooled into thinking that he can successfully pursue the study of Orthodox theology without simultaneously following the patristic way of purification of the passions.[28]

Only through this process of purification and intense introspection can one be adequately prepared to be sent out to serve the Lord and His Holy Church. Elder Paisius of Mount Athos offers this advice to Orthodox seminarians of today: "Endeavor as much as you can to become a good priest by working on yourself. Then you will see that your parishioners will start becoming better persons, without your even exerting yourself for them. Therefore, it is worth exerting yourself, working on yourself. Such is quiet work upon your neighbor."[29] Such words recall the popular saying of St. Seraphim of Sarov, "Have peace in your heart and thousands around you will be saved."[30]

---

[27] St. Gregory Palamas, *Defense of the Hesychasts* 3. 1. 32; trans. N. Gendle, New York, 1983, p. 87; Συγγράμματα 1, ed. P. Chrestou, p. 644. Cf. St. Gregory of Nyssa, *The Life of Moses* 2. 160-161; *Gregorii Nyssenii Opera* 7. 1, ed. W. Jaeger, pp. 85-86.

[28] For further reading on the purification of the passions, refer to A. Keselopoulos, *Passions and Virtues*, South Canaan, 2004 and D. Staniloae, *Orthodox Spirituality*, South Canaan, 2003.

[29] Quoted from *Orthodox Tradition*, vol. 18, no. 3, 2001, p. 35.

[30] Cf. H. Boosalis, *The Joy of the Holy*, South Canaan, 1993, pp. 83-85.

From these words of Elder Paisius, one gets the sense that if the student really wants to pursue Orthodox theology in the way of his Fathers before him, he must come to the realization that there is work to do first on himself, and not just in the academic arena.

We have to become conscious of our need for an inner spiritual transformation before we consider ourselves worthy of, or even ready for, this calling to study Orthodox patristic theology. It is our Fathers who are the authentic theologians of our Church *par excellence*. Are we properly prepared to have the Church Fathers as our teachers, our mentors, our spiritual guides?

Just as every believer confesses his unworthiness to receive Holy Communion, and just as every priest confesses his unworthiness during the celebration of every Divine Liturgy, we too, in a similar fashion, should confess our own unworthiness to follow in the theological footsteps of our holy Church Fathers.

Theology as Repentance

Yet it is not enough simply to confess our unworthiness. We must feel it. We must sense it. We must become repulsed by the stench of our sins, to the point where it leads to genuine repentance. Only then do we really begin to become students of the Fathers: "Without the spirit of repentance, without the experience of true obedience, one cannot become a true theologian or priest, that is, a person capable of teaching others the true Christian way."[31]

---

[31] Archim. Sophrony, *Words of Life*, p. 35.

The study of theology thus begins with a deep dark descent into the secret chambers of our heart. When done properly, and always with the aid of our spiritual father, what we find there can be quite frightening. It is not a pleasant experience. We encounter the enormity of our passions, the lusts of our flesh, our anger toward our neighbor and the pride of our ego: "Blessed is the man who knows his own weakness, because this knowledge becomes to him the foundation, the root, and the beginning of all goodness."[32]

Such a decent entails many spiritual trials and temptations, and these in turn demand much patience and humility. "God does not grant a great gift without a great trial,"[33] writes St. Isaac the Syrian.

According to Elder Vasileios of Iviron Monastery on Mount Athos, "In spiritual life, the aim of all struggle and ascetic practice is to lead man to humility, to free him from the ego that torments him, so that he can receive the grace of the Holy Spirit. All this struggle is necessary, not for us to ascend spiritually, but for us to descend, to be humbled."[34]

Before ascending to the heights of theology, we must therefore first descend into the dark abyss of our heart. This is the way of humility, one of the primary virtues that attracts the grace of the Holy Spirit.

---

[32] St. Isaac the Syrian, *The Ascetical Homilies* 8, trans. Holy Transfiguration Monastery, Boston, 1984, p. 67.
[33] St. Isaac the Syrian, *The Ascetical Homilies* 42, ibid., p. 209.
[34] Archim. Vasileios, *Hymn of Entry*, trans. E. Brière (Theokritoff), Crestwood, 1984, p. 102.

Without humility, we are left to the devices of our own words and human wisdom, bereft of the divine power of the Holy Spirit: "And my speech and my preaching were not with persuasive words of human wisdom, but in demonstration of the Spirit and of power."[35]

Without a proper understanding of the genuine need for humility, there is no sense in preparing to become an Orthodox priest. Without a willingness and desire to struggle against one's passion of pride, there is no sense in studying Orthodox theology. One must first strive to acquire the virtue of humility. True theology, therefore, commences only with a life lived in true repentance. This requires a change in our very way of life, with a focus no longer on our own self-interests, on our own strengths, abilities and accomplishments, on our own individual opinions and ideas.

Our focus must now be on God and on our brothers, and on *their* strengths, abilities and accomplishments, and on whatever they may have to offer the Lord in the service of His Holy Church. One of the most succinct definitions of true humility can be found in the writings of St. Dorotheos of Gaza: "Humility is to hold my brother to be wiser than myself, and in all things to rate him higher than myself, and simply ... to put oneself below everyone."[36]

---

[35] 1 Cor. 2. 4.
[36] St. Dorotheos of Gaza, *Discourses* 2, trans. E. Wheeler, Kalamazoo, 1977, p. 98; PG 88, 1645C.

St. Silouan of Mount Athos likewise writes, "We must count ourselves the worst of all men, and then the Lord by the Holy Spirit will give us to know the humility of Christ."[37] This is true 'μετάνοια', the Greek word for repentance, which when translated literally implies 'a change in one's mind'.[38] This is true humility as the Fathers understand the term. This is how Orthodox theology becomes a new way of life.

Our outlook toward ourselves and our brothers must take on a completely different perspective. If such an attitude towards ourselves and our brothers is required by our Church Fathers for all those seeking to live genuine Orthodox spiritual lives, how much more would they require it of us, who are being called to become their students and indeed the inheritors of their teachings, and not only for our own spiritual growth, but in order to teach others? We should take heed of the words of the Apostle James, the Brother of our Lord, "My brethren, let not many of you become teachers, knowing that we shall receive a stricter judgment."[39]

Many of us are well practiced in the art of covering up our own sins and spiritual shortcomings, even from our own eyes, while being very aware of those of our brothers around us. This makes it easier to 'talk' about theology. For some it is even fun and entertaining to do so.

---

[37] Archim. Sophrony, *Saint Silouan the Athonite*, trans. R. Edmonds, Essex, 1991, p. 277. See also pp. 300 and 308.
[38] *A Patristic Greek Lexicon*, p. 855. Cf. Rom 12. 2, "Be transformed by the renewing of your mind."
[39] James 3. 1.

It may not be so difficult to offer witty remarks, to write persuasive papers and to entice others to share in one's own opinions on subjects of 'theology'. Elder Vasileios observes, "Today ... we often take theology out of the theanthropic mystery of the Church in which it was sung by the Fathers. We transfer it to the field of mere academic discussions, where each person remaining an individual, an isolated authority, states his opinions and goes his way. The resultant 'theology', however, is not the very theology of the Church. If we disincarnate theology and transfer it, as a mere opinion, to a round table for discussion, it is wrong and untenable to say that this is 'the truth'."[40]

It is not enough, therefore, simply to talk theology. What is required of the Orthodox student is to live it. We must transform our individual and isolated way of life and lead it into the catholic fullness of the life of the Orthodox Church, where we begin to hand ourselves over to the grace of the Holy Spirit.

Orthodox theology is not concerned about discussions and debates for their own sake. The concern is the spiritual life of the human person:

> How frequently the Lord would stop people who wanted to start a 'theological' conversation with Him. They ask, 'Will those who are saved be few?' and the Lord replies, 'Strive to enter by the narrow door' (Luke 13. 23-24) ...

---

[40] Archim. Vasileios, *Hymn of Entry*, p. 32.

In a moment He leads the conversation into the field of personal life, of true theology. In every case He is interested in the person, not in theological discussion as an isolated occupation remaining out of touch with life and with the very person who is speaking.[41]

The true way of theology entails a process of personal and spiritual growth.

Theology as Charismatic Experience

The significance of the personal growth of the student is directly related to the fundamental work of the grace of the Holy Spirit within Orthodox theological studies. In this light, Orthodox theology may be seen as 'charismatic' experience,[42] since true knowledge of God does not result from human endeavor alone. Ultimately it is a gift of the Holy Spirit. It is by the grace of the Holy Spirit that the theologian properly understands and correctly interprets the truths of the Orthodox Faith: "When man ... has been caught up by grace into a vision of Divine Light, he afterwards translates into theology the things he has seen and known. ... theology consists, not in the conjectures of man's reason or the results of critical research but in a statement of the life

---

[41] Archim. Vasileios, *Hymn of Entry*, pp. 32-33.
[42] Cf. Ecumenical Patriarch Bartholomew I, 'Orthodox Theology: Divine Charisma and Personal Experience' in *Theology Today*, vol. 61, no. 1 (April, 2004), pp. 7-13.

into which man has been introduced by the action of the Holy Spirit."[43]

There must be a conscious effort on the part of the theologian, not simply to call on, but to come to depend upon, the grace of the Holy Spirit. It is His guidance and His inspiration which are needed if one is to acquire a proper patristic understanding of theology. Many issues will be encountered that will take time, and demand much prayer and patience in order to be understood and slowly incorporated into one's own personal life.

A 'synergy' or co-operation must take place between the divine grace of the Holy Spirit and the human effort of the student. The student must always be mindful of the work of the Holy Spirit within the theological process. Orthodox theology is a synergy between God's grace and the ascetic efforts and reasoning abilities of man.

If one is to plug into this grace, the source of inspiration will be his participation in the life of the Church and in Holy Tradition. Indeed it is impossible to be taught the truths of Orthodox theology apart from one's participation in Holy Tradition. Vladimir Lossky defined Holy Tradition as "the life of the Holy Spirit in the Church, communicating to each member of the Body of Christ the faculty of hearing, of receiving, of knowing the Truth ..."[44]

---

[43] Archim. Sophrony, *Saint Silouan the Athonite*, p. 170.
[44] V. Lossky, *In the Image and Likeness of God*, Crestwood, 1985, p. 152.

The believer will arrive at the correct understanding of Gospel Truth only to the degree that he gives himself over to Holy Tradition through the Church's liturgical life of worship: "Outside the framework of the Divine Liturgy ... it is impossible to understand Orthodox faith and theology."[45] Holy Tradition, which encompasses all aspects of our ecclesial life, thus serves as the font through which the Lord pours forth His divine grace upon the members of His Church.

Theology as Participation in Divine Life

We see, then, that Orthodox students of theology are not called to 'know God' through an intellectual process and the use of logical arguments. We are called to 'know God' through *participation* in His divine life. We must 'put on Christ' and live the 'life in Christ' through participation in the life of His Holy Church. The Gospel of Christ is not about abstract truths. It is about a Person. We do not learn about God through abstract theological theories. We 'know God' when we experience Him as members of His Holy Body. Without this 'knowing', there is no true theology.

---

[45] Archim. Vasileios, *Hymn of Entry*, p. 32. Refer also to A. Calivas, "The person called to be a theologian is formed by the faith of the Church and is inspired, illumined and taught by the Holy Spirit who dwells in her. Theology is both learned and taught in the Church, and especially in the context of her worship, in which the faithful people encounter the living God." *Essays in Theology and Liturgy*, vol. 1 (*Theology: The Conscience of the Church*), Brookline, 2002, p. 17.

Again, Orthodox theology is not simply the product of scholarly achievements alone. It comes from living and experiencing the life in Christ, which is based on one's sacramental, liturgical, ascetic and prayerful participation in the life of the Church, and this in itself transcends the limitations of human logic.

The fullness of this life is inexhaustible, because the God whom we encounter and His love that we experience are divine and thus inexhaustible. This is why our theology can never be restricted to a scholastic system of philosophical axioms. The student must always bear in mind that he is dealing with ultimate Truth, indeed Truth with a capital 'T'.

The utter reality of God's love for us and the true significance of His Incarnation and its impact on our daily lives will never be fully understood in this age. As the Apostle Paul teaches, "For now we see in a mirror, dimly, but then face to face. Now I know in part, but then I shall know just as I also am known."[46]

Knowledge of God, for our Church Fathers, is not limited to a logical or discursive understanding that depends upon the abilities of one's brain. True knowledge of God is based on the experience of participation in His divine life and love. It is knowing—indeed living —the love of Christ, or as St. Paul says, "to know the love of Christ which passes knowledge; that you may be filled with all the fullness of God."[47]

---

[46] 1 Cor. 13. 12.
[47] Eph. 3. 19.

Elder Sophrony also refers to this patristic understanding of knowledge of God with these words: "The human spirit is led by the Spirit of Christ to knowledge of God, existential knowledge, so that the very word 'knowledge' denotes, not abstract intellectual assimilation, not rational understanding, but entry into divine being, communion in being."[48] The summit of theology is thus an existential and an experiential encounter with the personal God.

St. Symeon the New Theologian reiterates the crucial importance of such an experience, especially for those who are called to teach others:

> Those who simply teach do not gain the Lord's blessing. It is for those who have first practiced the commandments and so have deserved to see and contemplate the shining and brilliant radiance of the Spirit within themselves. For with this vision, this knowledge and power, the Spirit instructs them fully in all that they must speak of and teach others. So, as I have said, all those who try to teach must first of all become *students* lest they wander off and lose themselves by speaking of things outside their experience. This is the fate of men who trust in themselves.[49]

---

[48] Archim. Sophrony, *Saint Silouan the Athonite*, p. 217.
[49] St. Symeon the New Theologian, *The Practical and Theological Chapters* 1. 4, trans. J. McGuckin, Kalamazoo, 1982, pp. 33-34 [emphasis mine].

Knowledge of God is beyond us, yet He has indeed revealed Himself to us. He leaves it up to us to react and respond to this sometimes fearful revelation. 'Knowing' God does not mean simply speaking about Him; it means experiencing him; it means encountering Him. According to St. Gregory Palamas, "Insofar as theology is removed from this vision of God in light and is separated from conversing with God, to such an extent it is cut off from perceiving that for which it was appointed; for to speak about God and to meet God are not the same thing."[50]

Theology involves a never-ending process of spiritual growth. While we are dealing with unchanging truth and the certainty of dogmatic definitions, we must constantly acknowledge that we will always encounter elements of the mysterious and unknowable in our pursuit of theology. We must learn to accept and deal with the fact that there will be many questions where there is no final and definitive answer.

Our Lord has not revealed all the secrets of the universe to us, nor have the Church Fathers provided us with a handbook wherein the student can conveniently look up the answer to every theological question. For some, this can be somewhat frustrating.

One must learn to become comfortable with *not* knowing certain theological truths and be content with simply living these truths in one's daily life as one progresses, by the grace of God, in the participation of

---

[50] St. Gregory Palamas, *Defense of the Hesychasts* 1. 3. 42; trans. Hieromonk Alexios (Trader) and H. Boosalis, in *Passions and Virtues* by A. Keselopoulos, South Canaan, 2004, p. 203; Συγγράμματα 1, ed. P. Chrestou, p. 453.

the life in Christ. The Lord does not ask us simply to learn theology; He invites us to live it. The study of theology, therefore, is a process wherein the student must come to accept the way of life that is required of him.

To summarize then, just what *is* Orthodox theology? It is a spiritual process. It is the transfiguration of the human person through a life of prayer, purification, repentance and ascetic struggle. It is a synergy between God and man. It is a charismatic experience. It is participation in divine grace. Orthodox theology is a way of life.

Chapter Three

ORTHODOX DOGMA: AN EASTERN APPROACH TO THE STUDY OF DOGMATIC THEOLOGY

This chapter deals with the scope of Orthodox dogmatic theology, discussing such topics as its goals, its purpose and the range of its activities. First we will provide some preliminary definitions and clarify other introductory issues.

Preliminary Definitions

Dogmatic theology is the study of the official doctrinal teachings of the Church. It deals with the formulation and presentation of the dogmas of the Church. The word 'dogma' (δόγμα) is defined as a "tenet or doctrine authoritatively put forth; prescribed doctrine; an established belief or principle."[51]

---

[51] *Webster's College Dictionary*, New York, 2001, p. 364.

The term is derived from the ancient Greek verb δοκέω (δοκεῖν in the infinitive) which means 'to hold an opinion' or 'to think', and often with the connotation of 'that which seems good'.[52] In the New Testament, the word occurs in the Book of Acts in reference to the missionary activity of Sts. Paul and Timothy: "And as they went through the cities, they delivered to them the decrees (δόγματα) to keep, which were determined by the apostles and elders at Jerusalem."[53]

A dogma is thus a "fixed belief"[54] or formal theological doctrine held in common by members of the Church. These, however, are dictionary definitions. For Orthodox theologians, the term 'dogma' has deeper significance.

Elder Vasileios writes, "Dogma is the expression of the mystical life of the Church, the formulation in the Holy Spirit of the Trinitarian experience into which the whole man is baptized through the Church. Dogmas do not concern just the experts; they give guidance and are a prerequisite for life; they lead unerringly to the fullness of life in the Holy Spirit."[55]

---

[52] *A Patristic Greek Lexicon*, p. 378. Grammatically, 'dogma' (δόγμα) derives from 'δέδογμαι', which is a variation of the perfect tense, passive voice of 'δοκέω'; see *Λεξικὸ Ρημάτων τῆς Ἀρχαίας Ἑλληνικῆς Γλώσσας*, ed. P. Giannakopoulos, Athens, 1995, p. 328.
[53] Acts 16. 4.
[54] *A Patristic Greek Lexicon*, p. 377.
[55] Archim. Vasileios, *Hymn of Entry*, p. 19.

Blessed Justin Popovich also sees this direct link between dogma and true life. He emphasizes the importance of the relationship between dogma and one's proper perspective of the new life in Christ: "The sacred dogmas are the eternal and saving divine Truths because they are based upon the life-giving power of the divine Holy Trinity, from which all of the power of the new life in Christ is derived. The new life in Christ is [woven] completely from the dogmas, from the dogmatic truths of the revelation of God."[56] Both of these writers obviously see a direct connection between Orthodox dogma and Orthodox spiritual life. There cannot be one without the other.

Vladimir Lossky states that one's experience of the life in Christ will necessarily reflect the dogmas one holds. Conversely, the dogmas one holds will reflect one's experience of Christ. More simply put, dogma expresses devotion, and devotion expresses dogma. Discussing the Church's doctrine and devotion to the Mother of God, Lossky writes, "Here dogma should throw light on devotion, bringing it into contact with the fundamental truths of our faith; whereas devotion should enrich dogma with the Church's living experience."[57]

Metropolitan Hierotheos of Nafpaktos refers to dogmas as the expression of the life of the Church and considers them as boundaries. He also mentions their therapeutic nature: "It is for this reason, in fact, that

---

[56] J. Popovich, *Orthodox Faith and Life in Christ*, trans. A. Gerostergios, Belmont, 1994, p. 201.
[57] V. Lossky, *In the Image and Likeness of God*, p. 196. Cf. G. Florovsky, *Creation and Redemption*, Belmont, 1976, p. 173.

dogmas are called boundaries, which draw the lines between truth and error ... dogmas are the way and the medicines which we receive to be cured and reach divinization ... dogmas are the expression of the life of the Church."[58]

This aspect of dogmas as medicines by which we are cured and reach divinization (which is also referred to as theosis, deification or glorification) is of central significance to Orthodox Tradition. As a result of the Fall, *all* mankind suffers from spiritual illness.

From the ecclesial perspective, *every* man is sick and is suffering. There is not one who is spiritually 'normal' or healthy, except of course for the Saints, who have attained theosis—that is to say, who have been granted the gift of participation in divine life, for which man was originally created: "So in the Church we are divided into the sick, those undergoing therapeutic treatment, and those—saints—who have already been healed."[59] Orthodox theology thus provides a therapeutic method or process whereby one is healed through the purification of passions, experiences divine illumination, and ultimately attains theosis: "Theology is a therapeutic treatment. It cures man."[60]

---

[58] Metro. Hierotheos, *The Illness and Cure of the Soul in the Orthodox Tradition*, trans. E. Mavromichali, Levadia, 1993, p. 16.
[59] Metro. Hierotheos, *Orthodox Psychotherapy*, trans. E. Williams, Levadia, 1994, p. 30.
[60] Metro. Hierotheos, *The Illness and Cure of the Soul*, p. 69.

Herein lies the importance of Orthodox dogma. The aim of Orthodox dogma is not to subject man to the confines of a particular religious philosophy. Rather, dogma leads to therapy.[61] It leads to the cure of fallen man.[62]

However, it must be emphasized that dogmas in themselves do not heal man; they simply show the way. An intellectual acceptance of the *letter* of dogma is not an automatic guarantee of being healed. It is not a matter of simply agreeing with the wording; one must *experience* the spirit of Orthodox dogma by means of a living faith within the therapeutic life of the Church.[63]

Dogmas are truly meaningful "only for those who have encountered the Living Christ ... and are dwelling by faith in Him, in His body, the Church."[64] Cut off from this ecclesial experience, dogmas remain dry, empty, and abstract formulae.

---

[61] See J. Romanides, Δογματική καὶ Συμβολικὴ Θεολογία τῆς Ὀρθοδόξου Καθολικῆς Ἐκκλησίας, vol. 1, Thessaloniki, 2004, pp. 9-45.

[62] Refer to the works of Metro. Hierotheos of Nafpaktos, *Orthodox Psychotherapy*, and *The Person in the Orthodox Tradition*, Levadia, 1998, which are more scholarly studies, as well as his *The Illness and Cure of the Soul in the Orthodox Tradition*, which is presented as a dialogue between a priest and a small group of parishioners.

[63] See J. Romanides, Δογματική καὶ Συμβολικὴ Θεολογία, vol. 1, pp. 52-58.

[64] G. Florovsky, *Bible, Church and Tradition: An Eastern Orthodox View*, Vaduz, 1987, p. 109.

Dogmas are thus not ends in themselves; they are guides that point the way toward the therapy of authentic spiritual life in Christ. The purpose of Orthodox dogma is to heal. Heretical teachings, on the other hand, always arise from those who do not know or follow, or who have deviated from, the Church's therapeutic process. Whenever a heretical innovation is manifested within the Church, it results directly from the fact that the one introducing this innovation has neither a correct understanding of dogma, nor has he truly experienced the proper therapeutic process of the Church.[65] This is what led the Church to define her dogmas—in order to protect and preserve the truth of her therapeutic method of purification, illumination, and theosis.

In this light, Professor Georgios Mantzaridis considers dogmas as "pointers to life,"[66] and he refers to them as "boundaries" that safeguard against heretical errors: "By its dogma, the Church has marked out the boundaries [σύνορα] in relation to the deviations which have appeared at different times, and therefore, the Church's dogmas are called 'definitions' [ὅροι]."[67] Dogmas are thus definitions which have been proclaimed by the Church in order to guard her members from the errors of heretical teachings.

---

[65] See J. Romanides, Δογματικὴ καὶ Συμβολικὴ Θεολογία, vol. 1, pp. 40-45 and 57.
[66] See G. Mantzaridis, *Orthodox Spiritual Life*, trans. K. Schram, Brookline, 1994, pp. 42-56.
[67] G. Mantzaridis, *Orthodox Spiritual Life*, p. 47.

The term heresy is derived from the Greek word αἱρέω (αἱρεῖν in the infinitive) which means 'to take for oneself' or 'to choose.'[68] Heresy has the connotation of picking or choosing what one wants to believe while disregarding the fullness of the authoritative theological doctrines of the Church. While the Fathers expressed their common ecclesial experience of the living God through their shared teachings, the heresiarchs ('arch-heretics'—the instigators of heretical movements), who separated themselves from this experience, arrived at their misguided conclusions individually—on their own.

Teachers of heresies who have not accepted the Church's judgment on their teachings and are anathematized by the Church and thus excommunicated, yet continue with such teachings, may be likened to medical doctors who experiment with dangerous new drugs by prescribing them to their patients even after such drugs have been officially banned. Metropolitan Hierotheos observes:

> The anathemas cannot be regarded as philosophical ideas and as states of hatred for other doctrines, but as medical actions. First of all the heretics by the choice which they have made have ended in heresy and in their departing from the teaching of the Church ...

---

[68] *Greek-English Lexicon*, ed. Liddell and Scott, Oxford, 1968, p. 42.

In this way they demonstrate that they are ill and in reality are cut off from the Church. Excommunication thus has the meaning of showing the separation of the heretic from the Church. The holy Fathers by this action of theirs confirm the already existing condition, and besides this, they help ... Christians to protect themselves from the heresy-illness.[69]

The danger of heresy is that it does not work; it does not *heal*. It leads to misinterpretation and misunderstanding. It contests and contradicts the Church's apostolic teaching of man's salvation and sanctification in Christ. Heresy is basically a deviation, indeed a delusion, that denies the apostolic truth upheld in the Church's dogmas. In the words of Elder Sophrony, "Any and every dogmatic error will inevitably reflect on one's spiritual life."[70]

The aim of dogma is not to intellectually explain the theological teachings of the Church so that they can be better understood from a philosophical point of view; rather the aim is to defend against heretical teachings that lead away from the Church's experience of deification in Christ. In this light, dogmas have a double perspective. On one hand, they point to and *give guidance* toward the full and abundant life that Christ

---

[69] Metro. Hierotheos, *The Mind of the Orthodox Church*, trans. E. Williams, Levadia, 1998, pp. 223-224.
[70] Archim. Sophrony, *Saint Silouan the Athonite*, p. 230.

promises to his disciples;[71] on the other hand, they *serve as safeguards* against heretical deviations that lead one away from the fullness of the life in Christ, which is found only in His Body, the Holy Church.

The Soteriological Concern

As we have said, the Church officially formulated her dogmas as a result of the need to counter heretical teachings. For example, the Church has always worshipped the One God, the Holy Trinity—Father, Son, and Holy Spirit. She has always preached, taught and baptized in the name of the One God—Father, Son, and Holy Spirit—from the very beginning of her existence, without having the need for an officially formulated and authoritatively proclaimed Trinitarian doctrine.

However, it was the heresy of Arianism, that taught that the Son was not truly God by nature, which led the bishops of the Church to gather together in 325 at the First Ecumenical Council of Nicea; and it was the rise of the Pneumatomachians or 'Spirit-fighters', who taught that the Holy Spirit likewise was not truly God by nature, that led to the Second Ecumenical Council of Constantinople in 381. At these two councils the Church officially proclaimed her teaching upholding the full divinity of both the Son and the Holy Spirit, which is summarized in the Nicene-Constantinopolitan Creed.

---

[71] See John 10. 10.

Throughout the first three centuries of her existence, the Church was content to simply *live* her life glorifying the Holy Trinity through her sacramental life of liturgical worship and ascetical life of prayer. Nothing really warranted or required an official formulation of an exact Trinitarian dogma. This is not to say that the Church did not have ample occasion to articulate her theological teachings outside of the immediate threat of heresy.

Such occasions, such as evangelism, preaching, and the instruction of her faithful, will be discussed later in more detail. However, without the danger of outright heresy, which attacked the very truth of the Gospel itself, these teachings did not require the assembly of hierarchs in a formal conciliar setting in order to officially and authoritatively proclaim them as 'dogmas' of the Church.

The Church did not formulate her dogmas for the sake of mere philosophical speculation, nor did the Fathers engage in theological discourse out of curiosity for abstract theoretical propositions. Rather, the Church was motivated by her concern to protect her faithful by defending her beliefs and practices against the threat of heretical teachings, and thus safeguard her apostolic experience of salvation and sanctification in the glorified and risen Christ: "All the development of the dogmatic battles which the Church has waged down the centuries appears to us, if we regard it from the purely spiritual standpoint, as dominated by the constant preoccupation which the Church has had to safeguard, at each moment of her history ... the possibility of attaining to the fullness of the mystical union."[72]

There was a *soteriological* concern which motivated the official formulation of Church dogmas (soteriology being the study of salvation). The Church was compelled to authoritatively proclaim her dogmas as a direct result of her need to refute various heresies, all of which lead away from her therapeutic experience of purification, illumination, and theosis in Christ.

Dogmas as Definitions

Fr. Georges Florovsky refers to dogma as a testimony of experience: "Dogma is the testimony ... about what has been seen and revealed, about what has been contemplated in the experience of faith—and this testimony is expressed in concepts and definitions. Dogma is ... a 'logical icon' of divine reality. And at the same time a dogma is a definition—that is why it's logical form is so important ... This is why the external aspect of dogma—its wording—is so essential."[73]

The importance of experience in relation to the Church's formulation of dogma cannot be overemphasized. It must be stressed that dogma presupposes experience. Dogmas express the living experience of the Church.[74] Only in the *experience* of the life in Christ do dogmas come alive. Furthermore, dogmas do not exhaust this experience.

---

[72] V. Lossky, *The Mystical Theology of the Eastern Church*, Crestwood, 1976, pp. 9-10.
[73] G. Florovsky, *Creation and Redemption*, p. 29.
[74] See G. Mantzaridis, *Orthodox Spiritual Life*, p. 47.

This experience of living the fullness of the life of Christ's Holy Church is much more inclusive and far-reaching than her dogmatic definitions.[75] Dogmas do not displace experience; they only seek to express it; seeking to express the inexpressible.

Nonetheless, the definitions themselves are also of paramount importance. In order to find the best possible way to convey the experience, the exact wording of dogmatic definitions become crucial, since dogmas are the guides, boundaries, and safeguards of the Church's experience of the life in Christ.

If this experience is lacking or disregarded, dogmas are reduced to abstract formulations; and if the doctrinal formulations are inaccurate or erroneous, they will lead to a misguided and incoherent experience: "The quest for dogmatic definitions is therefore, above all, a quest for terms. Precisely because of this the doctrinal controversies were a dispute over terms. One had to find accurate and clear words which could describe and express the experience of the Church."[76]

Fr. Meyendorff describes the antinomy involved in both the *necessity* as well as the *inability* of human language to express this experience:

> No civilization has ever lived through more discussions on the adequacy, or inadequacy, of words reflecting religious truths. The *homoousion* as distinct from the *homoiousion*; 'of two natures' or 'in two natures'; two wills or

---

[75] See G. Florovsky, *Creation and Redemption*, p. 29.
[76] Ibid., p. 30.

one will; ... procession 'from the Son' or 'through the Son'—these were issues debated by Byzantine Christians for centuries. It would seem, then, that the Greek Christian spirit consisted precisely in optimistically believing that human language is fundamentally adequate to express religious truth and that salvation depends upon the exact expression used to convey the meaning of the Gospel. Yet these same Greek Christians firmly confessed the incapacity of conceptual language to express the whole truth, and the incapability of the human mind to attain the essence of God. There was in Byzantium, therefore, an antinomy in the very approach to theology: God has really revealed Himself in Christ Jesus, and the knowledge of His Truth is essential to salvation, but God is also above the human intellect and cannot be fully expressed in human words.[77]

Again, the soteriological concern must be reiterated. The Fathers were forced to officially formulate doctrinal definitions only out of necessity. They were compelled to defend the Church's saving and sanctifying experience of life in Christ against the danger of heretical error, even though this experience was readily acknowledged as transcending the limitations of logic and language.

---

[77] J. Meyendorff, *Byzantine Theology*, New York, 1979, p. 5.

As another example, in his work titled *In Defense of the Hesychasts*, St. Gregory Palamas explains his attempt to define the Church's experience of deification in Christ:

> Deification is in fact beyond every name. This is why we, who have written much about *hesychia* (sometimes at the urging of the fathers, sometimes in response to the questions of the brothers) have never dared hitherto to write about deification. But now, since there is a necessity to speak, we will speak words of piety (by the grace of the Lord), but words inadequate to describe it. For even when spoken about, deification remains ineffable, and (as the Fathers teach us) can be given a name only by those who have received it.[78]

In this light, Lossky defines dogmas as "intelligible expressions of the reality which surpasses our mode of understanding."[79]

Still, the Church Fathers were aware that one incorrect preposition, or even the addition of one small 'iota' could have significant semantic implications and would thus certainly have an impact upon the proper expression of the Church's apostolic experience of the life in Christ.

---

[78] St. Gregory Palamas, *Defense of the Hesychasts* 3. 1. 32; trans. N. Gendle (under the title *The Triads*), New York, 1983, p. 87; Συγγράμματα vol. 1, p. 644.
[79] V. Lossky, *In the Image and Likeness of God*, p. 167.

Once these very carefully and precisely worded doctrinal definitions were finally and formally declared as official dogmas through the authority of the Church Councils, their very wording became, in fact, *unalterable*.[80] Furthermore, from the late fifth century, the emperors of Byzantium had to swear an oath at their coronation to defend the Orthodox Faith by upholding the dogmatic definitions of the first four, and later all seven, Ecumenical Councils.[81]

---

[80] For example, see the Preface to the Definition of Faith of the Council of Chalcedon as well as The Doctrinal Statement of the Seventh Ecumenical Council, in *Creeds and Confessions of Faith in the Christian Tradition*, vol. 1, ed. J. Pelikan and V. Hotchkiss, New Haven, 2003, pp. 177 and 235-237.

[81] See D. J. Geanakoplos, *Byzantium*, Chicago, 1984, p. 150, where a direct quote from an Imperial Oath to Preserve the Orthodox Creed is provided. This does not imply that the Church's doctrinal authority is restricted to the Seven Ecumenical Councils. For example, the councils of the fourteenth century which dealt with Palamite theology and formally endorsed the distinction between the divine essence and energies of God are of the utmost significance for Orthodox theology, and the Council of Constantinople in 879-880, which vindicated St. Photios the Great and annulled the decisions of the anti-Photian council of the previous decade, is even referred to by some Byzantine writers as 'the Eighth Ecumenical Council'; see *The Oxford Dictionary of Byzantium*, vol. 1, ed. A. P. Kazhdan, Oxford, 1991, p. 513, and the *Encyclopedia of Early Christianity*, ed. E. Ferguson, New York, 1990, p. 289. Cf. G. Florovsky: "The usual Eastern formula of 'Seven Ecumenical Councils' [tends] to *restrict* the Church's spiritual authority to the [first] eight centuries ... A *restrictive* commitment of the *Seven* Ecumenical Councils actually contradicts the basic principle of the *Living Tradition* in the Church. Indeed, *all* seven, but *not only* seven." *Aspects of Church History*, pp. 19-20.

The emperor St. Justinian the Great went even further. In 545 he declared the dogmatic definitions of the Ecumenical Councils (the first four up to his time) to be "sacred writings."[82]

We can now add another fundamental element to what characterizes the Church's dogmas. In addition to the already mentioned aspects of guides, boundaries, and safeguards, as well as the fact that they are testimonies of experience, and defined by the Church, we now add the characteristic that dogmas are also unalterable.

However, one must not be led into the erroneous view that dogmatic theology consists simply of the pursuit of a sterile exactitude in the letter of dogmatic formulation, for its own sake. Some of the more prominent Orthodox dogmatic manuals produced in the first half of the twentieth century can be characterized as reflecting such an approach. Even though these manuals refer to patristic sources, they are nonetheless based on Western scholastic methodology.

The Romanian Orthodox theologian, Fr. Dumitru Staniloae asserts:

> An inadequate theology is one that consists in a literal repetition of the words and formulae of the past. A damaging theology is one that remains fixed in the formulae of a past system and confuses these with revelation itself. . . .

---

[82] See J. Meyendorff, *The Byzantine Legacy in the Orthodox Church*, Crestwood, 1982, p. 47. Cf. *Novella* 131 of St. Justinian.

[Roman] Catholic theology did this for centuries in its repetition of the scholastic formulae, and sometimes even Orthodox theologians have done this, comfortably repeating the by-now opaque formulae of certain nineteenth-century manuals influenced by scholasticism, and making them into infallible criteria of judgment for Orthodoxy. This was a theology that hindered any spiritual revival and any spiritual progress, a theology devoid of all dynamic meaning and reflecting a static and exterior order which it continued to think of as perfect.[83]

As an example, Professor Christos Yannaras sees such a problem with Christos Androutsos and his book, *Dogmatics of the Orthodox Eastern Church* (published in 1907). He goes so far as to say that this book has "incarnated all the possible influences from the West."[84] He also criticizes the three volume work by Panayiotis Trembelas titled *Dogmatics of the Orthodox Catholic Church* (1959-1961), which he describes, again in strong language, as "a dogmatic system that is

---

[83] D. Staniloae, *The Experience of God*, trans. I. Ionita and R. Barringer, Brookline, 1994, p. 88. For further reading on Western influence on Modern Greek thought and theology see C. Yannaras, *Orthodoxy and the West*, Brookline, 2006. For Western influences on Russian theology see G. Florovsky, *Aspects of Church History*, pp. 157-182.

[84] C. Yannaras, 'Theology in Present-Day Greece', *SVTQ*, 16. 4, 1972, p. 199. For further reading on the theology of Androutsos see C. Yannaras, *Orthodoxy and the West*, pp. 202-206.

totally foreign to the spirit of the Eastern Fathers."[85] As he correctly observes, "Orthodox dogmatic theology is primarily concerned with fidelity to the exactitude of dogma *but at the same time* with the expression of the theological spirit and attitude of the Fathers, which was an *attitude of life* and *not* a matter of scholastically correct formulation."[86]

A strict and systematic formulation of rational propositions *apart* from the ecclesial encounter with the person of Christ can only foster the repetition of meaningless formulae with little or no bearing on one's spiritual life. According to Fr. Staniloae, "Theology will be effective if it stands always before God and helps the faithful to do the same in their every act: to see God through the formulae of the past, to express him through the explanations of the present, to hope and to call for the advancement towards full union with him in the life to come."[87]

---

[85] Ibid., p. 200. For further reading on the theology of Trembelas, see C. Yannaras, *Orthodoxy and the West*, pp. 206-216.
[86] Ibid., p. 201 [emphasis mine].
[87] D. Staniloae, *The Experience of God*, p. 93.

The Danger of Systematization

Having discussed these basic preliminary points, we must address a further issue. When teaching courses in dogmatic theology, there lies latent the danger of systematization. In the attempt to provide a clear-cut, concise, and formal thematic presentation of the doctrinal teachings of the Church, there is a temptation to divide and isolate one field from another. This tendency to over-compartmentalize the various branches of dogmatic theology, as if each unit stands apart separate on its own, must always be avoided. As Elder Sophrony states, "The Church's dogmatic confession constitutes an organic unity and integrality such as cannot arbitrarily be split up into sections."[88]

Fr. John Chryssavgis also observes, "It would be incorrect to overstress the division of theology into various fields or branches—biblical, historical, systematic and pastoral. Such divisions would only be justified for practical purposes, but the underlying unity of Orthodox theology must at all times be affirmed."[89]

This is why the study of dogmatic theology often exposes itself to the danger of being dissected into a number of different '-ologies'—which can lead to the *sterility* of an academic science separated from spiritual life, rather than the *virility* of ecclesial vision focused on the glorified Christ.

---

[88] Archim. Sophrony, *Saint Silouan the Athonite*, p. 230.
[89] J. Chryssavgis, *The Way of the Fathers*, Thessaloniki, 1998, p. 83.

The study of dogmatic theology for purposes of academic science alone falls outside the scope of the proper patristic perspective. In fact, the term 'dogmatic theology' would in itself sound strange to the ears of the Church Fathers. In all truth, for them there was no such thing as 'dogmatic theology'.

For the Fathers, such a subject simply did not exist. Theology was not something they studied, composed, or lectured on. It was an *experience* that they *lived*. They would reject any attempt to fragment their experience of the life in Christ into various scientific branches for academic study.

Such a scholastic division is foreign to the mind of the Fathers. For them theology was a way of life that one might comment on in order to instruct others, and certainly defend if need be; yet they would be reluctant to divide it up according to separate fields of study merely for the sake of academic analysis: "Not that a rational deductive process was completely eliminated from theological thought; but it represented for the [Fathers] the lowest and least reliable level of theology. The true theologian was the one who saw and experienced the content of his theology."[90] St. Basil the Great teaches succinctly, "Let us prefer the simplicity of faith to the demonstrations of reason."[91] The point is that theology must be pursued together with the *experience* of living faith.

---

[90] J. Meyendorff, *Byzantine Theology*, p. 9.
[91] St. Basil the Great, *Hexaemeron* 1. 10, trans. B. Jackson, NPNF, second series, vol. 8, Grand Rapids, 1989, p. 57. Cf. Clement the Alexandrian, *Stromata* 2. 4.

According to Elder Sophrony, "Academic theology [when] combined with living faith affords blessed results. But it can easily degenerate into abstract theory, and cease to be what we see in the lives of the Apostles, Prophets, Fathers—the direct action of God in us."[92] Dogmatic theology, therefore, is not concerned simply with the systematic study of abstract theoretical definitions, but rather with first *living*, and only then with *expressing*, the Church's experience of her mystical life in Christ.

This is not to imply that the Eastern Fathers never produced any systematic writings. One has only to look at *The Great Catechetical Oration* of St. Gregory of Nyssa, as well as the classic *Exact Exposition of the Orthodox Faith* by St. John Damascene, among other patristic writings, to see that this is not the case. Still, for the Fathers, the impetus for their writings was based on their ecclesial experience of the glorified Christ, and not on a desire for a systematic study for its own sake.[93] And there are far fewer systematic theologies written by Orthodox theologians to this day than there are by Western theologians.

When one approaches the study of the dogmas of the Church from a purely scientific perspective, devoting himself to scholastic methodology and criteria, one leaves himself open to the tendency to seek after systematic formulations for their own sake, which is alien

---

[92] Archim. Sophrony, *On Prayer*, p. 63.
[93] Cf. J. Meyendorff, "The East was less prone than the West to conceptualize or to dogmatize this unity of tradition. It preferred to maintain its faithfulness to the 'mind of Christ' through the liturgy of the Church." *Byzantine Theology*, p. 128.

to the ecclesial ethos with which Orthodox dogmas are organically bound. There is the danger of a divorce between doctrine and experience.[94]

The study of dogma can easily degenerate into a science of abstract propositions disconnected from any direct and intimate contact with the living experience of the Church. It can also become completely reduced from the truth into purely ethical teachings. Professor Anestis Keselopoulos writes:

> Such a division of ethics from dogma ... even for the sake of method and organization, is unknown in Orthodox tradition. And it is precisely in this artificial partitioning where we encounter the drama of scholastic theology that has unfolded in the West, and not infrequently has also affected Orthodox theological thought. This segregation has been fatal, since it fights against the very truth of life. Dogma expresses the Church's mystical life. Dogma puts in divinely inspired words the Trinitarian experience, wherein man finds the true core of his being.[95]

---

[94] Cf. A. Schmemann, "The goal of liturgical theology ... is to overcome the fateful divorce between theology, liturgy and piety —a divorce which ... has had disastrous consequences for theology as well as for liturgy and piety ... It deprived theology of its living source and made it into an intellectual exercise for intellectuals. It deprived piety of its living content and term of reference." *Of Water and the Spirit*, Crestwood, 1974, p. 12.

[95] A. Keselopoulos, *Passions and Virtues*, trans. Hieromonk Alexios (Trader) and H. Boosalis, South Canaan, 2004, pp. 17-18.

One must not lose sight of the unified vision of theology as a whole. All branches of dogmatic theology are inter-connected, inter-dependent, and mutually inclusive. It is impossible to correctly discuss one branch of dogmatic theology without referring to others as well. For instance, one cannot study Christology without referring to Trinitarian theology, and to anthropology, soteriology, and ecclesiology as well. Such distinctions are helpful for didactic purposes, in that they facilitate the practical presentation and discussion of particular theological themes, topics, and terms. But these *distinctions* must not lead to *divisions*. The various branches of dogmatic theology should not be seen as isolated from one another in order to be examined as independent units.

An example of such a dissection in Roman Catholicism is a branch of dogmatic theology that deals with issues concerning the Blessed Virgin Mary. This field of study is referred to as 'Mariology'.[96] Such a term is unheard of in patristic writings since it seems to place any discussion of Panayia[97] apart from the person of Christ.[98] For the Church Fathers, any theological discussion pertaining to Panayia is always seen in its proper context of Christology, and thus of anthropology as well, since she is the model of man deified.

---

[96] Cf. *The New Catholic Encyclopedia*, Washington D. C., 1967, pp. 223-227.
[97] In Greek, the name *Panayia* (literally 'the All-holy') is a more prevalent, intimate, and informal way of referring to and calling upon the Theotokos, which is a more formal appellation.
[98] See N. Matsoukas, Δογματικὴ καὶ Συμβολικὴ Θεολογία, vol. 2, Thessaloniki, 1992, pp. 295-296.

Lossky provides an illustration of the more holistic vision of how the various branches of dogmatic theology are all inter-connected, especially as they relate to Panayia: "The Orthodox Church has not made Mariology into an independent dogmatic theme: it remains integral to the whole of Christian teaching, as an anthropological *Leitmotif*. Based on Christology, the dogma of the Mother of God has a strong Pneumatological accent; and ... it is inextricably bound up with ecclesiological reality."[99]

Thus we see how the various branches of dogmatic theology are all intricately intertwined. Such a holistic perspective springing forth from the ethos of ecclesial experience and the liturgical life in Christ is the proper patristic path for pursuing the study of dogma: "That is why there is basically no difference between 'ethos' and dogma. Dogma formulates the 'ethos' of the Church. Theology expresses the experience of salvation."[100] Fr. Meyendorff accurately summarizes our main concern regarding the danger of systematization:

> In any systematic presentation of theology, there is, therefore, a danger of forcing it into

---

[99] V. Lossky, *In the Image and Likeness*, p. 195. This is not to imply that Orthodox theologians avoid the term completely. Some Orthodox writers use the term 'Mariology' or even 'Theotokology' (Θεοτοκολογία) but always in an integrated and holistic Orthodox context, e.g., G. Florovsky, *Creation and Redemption*, pp. 171-173; Metro. Hierotheos, *The Feasts of the Lord*, Levadia, 2003, p. 23; and D. Tseleggidis, Ὀρθόδοξη Θεολογία καὶ Ζωή, Thessaloniki, 2005, p. 39.

[100] C. Yannaras, 'Theology in Present-Day Greece', p. 195.

the mold of rational categories foreign to its very nature. This is precisely what occurred in many textbooks of dogmatic theology which appeared in the Orthodox East after the eighteenth century which claimed to remain faithful to the theology of the Byzantine Fathers. They have been ably characterized by Fr. Florovsky as expressions of a 'Western captivity' of the Orthodox mind. For, it is not enough to quote an abundance of proof-texts from patristic or Byzantine authors: true consistency requires a unity of method and ... approach."[101]

This patristic perspective, seen through the prism of ecclesial experience, is paramount if one is to preserve the multifaceted experience of the life in Christ as a coherent and unified whole.

---

[101] J. Meyendorff, *Byzantine Theology*, p. 128.

The Need for a Creed

With these introductory remarks in mind, we proceed to the task at hand, which is to discuss the scope of dogmatic theology. What does dogmatic theology provide the Church? What is the range of its activities? What are its goals? What is its purpose? At the core of dogmatic theology is the Incarnation of the Word—the revelation of the living God to the world in the person of Jesus Christ: "God, who at various times and in various ways spoke in time past to the fathers by the prophets, has in these last days spoken to us by His Son."[102] The Incarnate Christ is both the *beginning* as well as the ultimate *end* of dogmatic theology. The Incarnate Word is the axis around which all of our theology revolves.

Orthodox theology is a completely Christ-centered experience: "We see the Word, we see the Father in the Holy Spirit; we see the Word, we see the Church; we see the Word, we see the communion of the saints; we see the Word, we see the mysteries of the Church."[103] This experience includes both the *reception* of this revelation within the life of the Church as well as its *assimilation* within the life of the believer.[104]

---

[102] Heb. 1. 1-2.

[103] J. Romanides, Πατερικὴ Θεολογία, p. 223.

[104] See G. Mantzaridis, "Ἡ Ὀρθόδοξη Θεολογία στὴν ἱστορία καὶ τὸ παρόν", in Σύναξη, vol. 92 (Oct.-Dec., 2004), p. 10.

The goal of dogmatic theology is to properly express and interpret the ecclesial experience of the reception and assimilation of this revelation. This revelation in Jesus Christ is also the epiphany of true and authentic human life, as it is made known and participated in through the ascetical, sacramental, and liturgical life of the worshipping Church.

Theology is not an option. The believer must come to comprehend the content of his Faith, not only to share it with others, but first to incorporate it within his own life. He thus comes to truly understand and appreciate his participation in the life in Christ within His holy Church. Theology provides the Church with the means of expressing and interpreting her experience of the life in Christ through the formulation of her doctrinal teachings. In this light, Professor Mantzaridis refers to theology as the "expression of the Church's *self-consciousness*."[105] Fr. Schmemann likewise writes:

> The Church *needs* theology ... theology is the conscience of the Church, her purifying self-criticism, her permanent reference to the ultimate goals of her existence. Deprived of theology, of its testimony and judgment, the Church is always in danger of forgetting and misinterpreting her own Tradition, confusing the essential with the secondary ... losing the perspective of her life.[106]

---

[105] Ibid. Cf. G. Florovsky, *Aspects of Church History*, p. 192 and *Creation and Redemption*, p. 40.
[106] A. Schmemann, 'Theology and Eucharist', *SVTQ*, 5. 4, 1961, pp. 11-12.

Dogmatic theology is thus the expression of the Church's *self-awareness*.

The Church has always been aware of her need to explain and expound her faith in Christ. The Lord asked His disciples, "'Who do men say that I, the Son of Man, am?' So they said, 'Some say John the Baptist, some Elijah, and others Jeremiah or one of the prophets'. He said to them, 'But who do you say that I am?' Simon Peter answered and said, 'You are the Christ, the Son of the living God'."[107]

Ever since that time the Church has been occupied with the task of not only *preserving*, but also *interpreting* her apostolic faith in the divinity of Christ. She had to *articulate the content* of her faith for those who were interested in learning about Christ; she had to *formulate the tenets* of her faith in order to instruct her catechumens; and she had to *defend the orthodoxy* of her faith against the threat of heretical deviations.

As the Church grew and expanded throughout the various regions of the Roman Empire, and throughout the world, the need arose to further elucidate her authentic and apostolic confession of faith. Not only for purposes of protecting her faithful, but also for evangelizing, catechizing, preaching, and teaching as well, the Church had to elaborate her beliefs in order to meet the demands of the various people she encountered.[108]

---

[107] Mt. 16. 13-16. Cf. B. Lohse, *A Short History of Christian Doctrine*, Philadelphia, 1985, p. 9.

[108] Cf. *Creeds and Confessions of Faith in the Christian Tradition*, vol. 1, pp. 3-37 and J. N. D. Kelly, *Early Christian Creeds*, New York, 1972, pp. 1-29.

It soon became apparent that the early apostolic confessions would need to be expanded to include other aspects of the Church's faith and life as well. From these apostolic confessions grew the ancient local creeds which addressed specific elements of the faith that called for further clarification, depending on the needs of each particular locality or region. While these local creeds all professed one and the same apostolic faith, they differed somewhat in their use of expressions and phraseology with regard to the degree of emphasis on specific details.

It was often thought that the variety of emphasis on particular details and their expansion from shorter affirmations to more elaborate creeds was due directly to the necessity of refuting specific heresies threatening a particular region. J. N. D. Kelly, in his work *Early Christian Creeds*, advises against over-emphasizing the anti-heretical nature of these ancient local creeds: "We should not rashly assume that it represents the only or the most important function of creeds, taking precedence over their original, and positive, function of setting forth the faith."[109] G. L. Prestige concurs: "The creeds of the Church grew out of the teaching of the Church; the general effect of heresy was rather to force old creeds to be tightened up than to cause fresh creeds to be constructed."[110] Regardless of the various theories relating to their formation, these ancient local creeds are important since they provided formal summaries of the central teachings of the early Church.

---

[109] J. N. D. Kelly, *Early Christian Creeds*, p. 65.
[110] G. L. Prestige, *Fathers and Heretics*, London, 1985, p. 3.

In regard to the appearance of the ancient local creeds, their *sacramental* setting, to which they were organically linked, is of primary significance. First and foremost, they must be seen in the light of their direct connection to the preparation of catechumens for Holy Baptism.[111] The Church required an official summary of her main beliefs. This was needed not only in order to *prepare* her catechumens with appropriate instruction, but also to *provide* them with an authoritative creedal statement—the formal recitation of which was, and still is, an integral element in the rite of their reception through Holy Baptism:

> It is important to stress ... that *creeds* and *symbols of faith* appeared and were used first in the context of baptismal preparation ... One of the most important parts of these [catechetical] instructions was the teaching of doctrine and the *mystagogy*, the explanation of the liturgical 'mysteries' ... [which concluded with] the solemn reading by the catechumen of the symbol of faith [i.e., the Creed] as the expression now of his own faith.[112]

Thus the early creeds became the standard by which one's faith was judged to be Orthodox and which determined one's reception into the Church.

---

[111] Cf. J. N. D. Kelly, *Early Christian Creeds*, pp. 30-61.
[112] A. Schmemann, *Of Water and the Spirit*, pp. 32-33.

In a more informal and less standardized way, there also arose another summary of the Church's main teachings, referred to as the Rule of Faith.[113] The phrase in Greek is ὁ κανών τῆς πίστεως, and in Latin, *regula fidei*. It may also be referred to as the Rule of Truth.[114] These phrases are sometimes translated into English as the Canon of Faith or the Canon of Truth.

The *Oxford Dictionary of the Christian Church* defines the Rule of Faith as "one of the names used to describe outline statements of Christian belief which circulated in the 2nd century Church and were designed to make clear the essential contents of the Christian faith, to serve as guides in the exegesis of Scripture ... and to distinguish the orthodox tradition from traditions to which heretics appealed."[115]

It is not clear what the precise wording of the Rule of Faith was. Intimately connected to the baptismal creeds, from which it should not be separated, the Rule of Faith is seen as their antecedent.[116] The Rule served a different function: it was not so much a firmly set *formula*, as were the creeds, but rather a series of summaries of the Church's essential teachings.

---

[113] Cf. St. Irenaeus, *Proof of the Apostolic Preaching* 3.
[114] Cf. St. Irenaeus, *Against Heresies* 1. 9. 4.
[115] The *Oxford Dictionary of the Christian Church*, ed. F. L. Cross and E. A. Livingston, 3rd ed., Oxford, 1997, p. 1424. Cf. J. N. D. Kelly, *Early Christian Creeds*, pp. 76-88.
[116] See *The Encyclopedia of Early Christianity*, ed. E. Ferguson, New York, 1990, pp. 804-805.

These less formal, yet still fundamental, summaries contained in the Rule of Faith can be seen as nascent doctrinal teachings of the early Church.[117] Although there could only be one and the same apostolic teaching shared by all Christian believers, the way in which its main points were taught and explained could take on different forms of expression. Different teachers had different ways of stating and elaborating these points. The Rule of Faith thus never acquired the same formalization as did the baptismal creeds.[118]

Regardless of its exact relationship with the early creeds, the Rule of Faith provided the Church with a tool for guiding her faithful toward the proper understanding of Holy Scripture, as well as for expressing and explaining the various points of her doctrinal teaching.

A final point regarding the Rule of Faith is its direct link to apostolic Tradition. The Rule of Faith was seen as apostolic not because the Apostles themselves had actually drafted its very wording, but because it stemmed from, and was grounded in, their original preaching, teaching, and tradition.[119] The faith that was passed on to each catechumen and which was solemnly confessed at every baptism thus incorporated the original faith as it was handed down from the Apostles to their immediate successors, who in turn not only preserved it, but also passed it on to those who followed them.

---

[117] See B. Lohse, *A Short History of Christian Doctrine*, p. 35.
[118] See *The Encyclopedia of Early Christianity*, p. 805.
[119] Cf. G. Florovsky, *Bible, Church and Tradition*, pp. 75-80.

In the words of St. Irenaeus:

> The Church ... though disseminated throughout the world, even to the ends of the earth, received from the apostles and their disciples the faith in one God the Father Almighty, the Creator of heaven and earth ... and in the one Jesus Christ, the Son of God ... and in the Holy Spirit ... The Church ... carefully guards this preaching and this faith which she has received, as if she dwelt in one house. She likewise believes these things as if she had but one soul and one and the same heart; she preaches, teaches, and hands them down harmoniously, as if she possessed but one mouth. For, though the languages throughout the world are dissimilar, nevertheless the meaning of the tradition is one and the same.[120]

This living Tradition is the bond that binds the same ecclesial experience of the Apostles with that of the Church Fathers, throughout the centuries, up to and including our own experience of the faith today.

---

[120] St. Irenaeus, *Against Heresies* 1. 10. 1-2, trans. D. J. Unger, New York, 1992, pp. 48-49.

Dogmas Do Not Develop

We have thus witnessed a gradual metamorphosis —from the apostolic confessions of the New Testament, to the initial formulation of the essential teachings of the ancient Church as found in the Rule of Faith, to the eventual standardization of the early baptismal creeds. All of these were significant steps toward the more complete formulation of the Church's dogmatic teachings which were ultimately, officially, and authoritatively declared as Orthodox dogma by conciliar decree.

However, this metamorphosis from confession to dogma does not include any notion of 'development' in the sense of a change or alteration in the Faith as it was handed down from the Apostles. According to Fr. Florovsky, "It is a total misunderstanding to speak of the 'development of dogma'. Dogmas do not develop; they are unchanging and inviolable, even in their external aspect—their wording ... As strange as it may appear, one can indeed say: dogmas arise, dogmas are established, but they do not develop."[121] There may have been an elaboration or clarification of terminology, but this does not mean that the fundamentals of the Faith changed over the course of time.

This is why it is incorrect to dissect the history of dogma into a succession of various stages of formulation that remain disconnected and separate from one another. There is an inherent unity and continuity that must continually be the focus of attention.

---

[121] G. Florovsky, *Creation and Redemption*, p. 30.

The Fathers never imagined they were *improving* or *changing* the content of the Apostolic Faith "which was once for all delivered to the saints."[122] They may have had to clarify or elaborate it with the use of certain terms, but they *never altered* its fundamental teaching. They did not approach the Truth as an evolving philosophic idea. They *experienced* the Truth, through a living and existential relationship with *the* Truth, who is a *person*—the Person of the Son of God.[123]

When the Fathers were forced to 'dogmatize', they were well aware of the fact that they were not adding anything new to the original apostolic experience. Their experience of the glorified Christ was the same as that of the Apostles: "Jesus Christ is the same yesterday, and today and forever."[124] It was only that this experience had to be protected from heretical misinterpretation—which called often for further clarification, and this the Fathers proceeded to do, but only *reluctantly*.[125]

The Fathers were so conscious of preserving whole and intact this apostolic experience that they prefaced their pronouncements, like that of the Fourth Ecumenical Council of Chalcedon, not only with the words "Following the Holy Fathers," but also with a declaration reaffirming the decisions of the previous ecumenical councils, and reiterating their original creeds.[126]

---

[122] Jude 3 (RSV).
[123] See John 14. 6.
[124] Heb. 13. 8.
[125] Cf. J. Meyendorff, *Byzantine Theology*, p. 10.
[126] See *Creeds and Confessions of Faith,* vol. 1, p. 177. Cf. J. Meyendorff, "Identical formulae are used by all the Byzantine Councils in the succeeding period." *Byzantine Theology*, p. 11.

In fact, in the Preface to their Definition of Faith, immediately after confirming, word for word, the original Nicene-Constantinopolitan Creed, the Fathers of Chalcedon added, "This wise and saving creed, the gift of divine grace, was sufficient for a perfect understanding and establishment of religion. For its teaching about the Father and the Son and the Holy Spirit is complete, and it sets out the Lord's becoming human to those who faithfully accept it."[127] It is obvious that Chalcedon never claimed to set forth or endorse a new dogma. Indeed, every council officially proclaimed that its doctrinal definitions were the same as the earlier decrees. Each affirmed that its decrees were not different from previous definitions.

As another example, the Doctrinal Statement of the Seventh Ecumenical Council states: "We neither diminish nor augment, but simply guard intact all that pertains to the catholic church ... we defend free from any innovations all the written and unwritten ecclesiastical traditions that have been entrusted to us."[128]

When they had to make dogmatic declarations, the Fathers were convinced that they did so not of themselves but only under the guidance of the Holy Spirit: "For it seemed good to the Holy Spirit, and to us ..."[129] They never saw any separation between their actions as the Church and the activity of the Holy Spirit.[130]

---

[127] *Creeds and Confessions of Faith in the Christian Tradition*, vol. 1, p. 177.
[128] Ibid., pp. 235-237.
[129] Acts 15. 28.
[130] Cf. G. Florovsky, *Bible, Church and Tradition*, pp. 93-103.

The Fathers never 'dogmatized' on their own but always in synergy with the grace of the Holy Spirit. As Fr. Florovsky writes, "It will be no exaggeration to suggest that Councils were never regarded as a canonical institution, but rather as occasional *charismatic events*."[131]

The Mind of the Fathers

This brings us to the crucial importance of adhering to our patristic tradition. This is a primary concern of Orthodox students of theology today: to pursue, participate in, and thus preserve the proper patristic perspective in all our theological endeavors. Being Orthodox means being true to the sources of our Tradition, and these sources are both apostolic and patristic.

Holy Tradition is the living expression of the ecclesial experience of the Apostles, Fathers, and Saints. Their lives and writings reflect their personal experience of the Church's therapeutic process of purification, illumination, and theosis. This is why our theology remains at the same time both biblical and patristic. To be patristic is to be apostolic in the sense of not only preserving, but also pursuing and participating in, the apostolic experience of the life in Christ as it is lived within His Holy Body, the Church.

Patristic theology is drawn from this experience as it is expressed, not exclusively in the apostolic writings contained in Holy Scripture, but more inclusively, as it is expressed throughout Holy Tradition as a whole.

---

[131] Ibid., p. 96.

From the patristic perspective, while there may be a distinction between Holy Tradition and Holy Scripture, they are never divided, isolated, nor opposed.

There is never a question of which one takes precedence over the other. Holy Tradition is the complete and all-encompassing expression of the apostolic experience of the life in Christ, while Holy Scripture is seen as one of its major components. Holy Tradition is apostolic because it expresses and reflects the fullness of the apostolic experience of Christ.

If we recall Lossky's definition of Holy Tradition as "the life of the Holy Spirit in the Church,"[132] we see how, within the life of the Body of Christ, these three factors are always held together in perfect harmony: the grace of the *Holy Spirit*, the experience of the *Apostles*, and the *Tradition* of our holy Fathers. To be patristic, therefore, is to be apostolic. To be patristic means being faithful to apostolic Tradition.[133] This is a basic aspect of what it means to be patristic.

Fr. Florovsky adds another dimension, which may be surprising for some. In his work *The Ways of Russian Theology*, he asserts that to be patristic also entails being 'Greek'—'Greek' *not* of course as it relates to the ethnic culture of the modern Greek nation, but 'Greek' in the sense of applying the Hellenistic mystical approach to spiritual life and the pursuit of theological knowledge, as well as the utilization and adaptation of Hellenic categories of thought:

---

[132] V. Lossky, *In the Image and Likeness*, p. 152.
[133] Cf. G. Florovsky, *Bible, Church and Tradition*, pp. 105-113.

Hellenism in the Church has been ... immortalized, having been incorporated into the very fabric of the reality of the Church as an eternal category of Christian existence ... in a certain sense, it is impossible to enter into the rhythm of the liturgical sacraments without some degree of mystical re-Hellenization. 'Hellenism' is more than merely a historical and transitional episode in the Church's life ... All of the temptation for a 'radical de-Hellenization' of Christianity ... cannot undermine the significance of the basic fact that the Good News and the theology of Christianity [were] expressed and fortified precisely in Hellenic categories. Patristics ... and Hellenism are ... attendant aspects of a single and indivisible design.[134]

Fr. Florovsky's observations on this intimate relationship between Hellenism and patristic theology arise from the context of his critique of the crisis of sixteenth century Russian theology, which was characterized by a falling away from patristic tradition.[135]

This break with patristic tradition was not limited to sixteenth-century Russia. It continued into the seventeenth, eighteenth, and even nineteenth centuries:

---

[134] G. Florovsky, *The Ways of Russian Theology*, vol. 2, Vaduz, 1987, p. 297. Cf. *Georges Florovsky: Russian Intellectual and Orthodox Churchman*, ed. A. Blaine, Crestwood, 1993, p. 155.
[135] See ibid., p. 294. Cf. *The Ways of Russian Theology*, vol. 1, Vaduz, 1979, pp. 26-32.

"The whole development of Russian theology since the seventeenth century, as taught in the schools, was but a dangerous borrowing from heterodox Western sources."[136] As was mentioned earlier, this influx of western influences—this western 'captivity'[137] of the Orthodox mind—also infiltrated the theological schools of modern Greece. And this is manifested in some of the dogmatic manuals published by the more prominent Greek theologians of the early to mid-twentieth century, as we have seen.[138]

This break with tradition was caused by the loss of the patristic approach to theology. Instead of the patristic and Hellenistic practice of contemplative experience, theology became an academic and intellectual pursuit.

---

[136] G. Florovsky, *Aspects of Church History*, p. 157.
[137] See ibid., p. 172.
[138] See footnote #83 above. The neo-patristic renaissance that could characterize the last half of the twentieth century and up to and including our own day, is generally considered to have been inaugurated with Fr. Florovsky's influential addresses delivered in Athens in 1936 at the First Congress of Orthodox Theologians, calling for Orthodox theology to return to its proper roots in patristic tradition; see *Georges Florovsky: Russian Intellectual and Orthodox Churchman*, p. 71. Another historic event leading the way back to a theology more correctly based on patristic sources and perspectives is the doctoral dissertation on ancestral sin submitted by Fr. John Romanides to the theological faculty of the University of Athens in 1957, which sparked heated debate, particularly with Prof. Trembelas; see A. Sopko, *The Theology of John Romanides*, Dewdney, 1998, pp. 11-45. One might also mention the influential contribution of the eminent patrologist, the late Prof. Panayiotis Chrestou of the University of Thessaloniki.

For some ancient Greek philosophical schools such as those of Pythagoras and the neo-Platonists, the acquisition of some forms of knowledge was considered a mystical experience. Through their intimate understanding of the ancient Greek philosophers, the Church Fathers were familiar with this contemplative, mystical and experiential approach to the acquisition of *divine* knowledge or knowledge of God.

For the Church Fathers, contemplation and asceticism served as the only authentic way of acquiring knowledge of divine truth. Clearly, the Church's ascetic approach to the knowledge of God through purification and illumination was not an innovation.

The Stoic philosophers, for example, emphasized that the way to such knowledge was through the purification or *katharsis* of the passions and the attainment of dispassion or *apatheia*—that is to say, through ascetic struggle and self-discipline. Although the patristic understanding of dispassion differed from that of the Stoics,[139] the Fathers nonetheless felt free to borrow such concepts and methods from the ancient Greek philosophers.

Yet they 'baptized' and 'transfigured' them in the light of the Church's experience of the life in Christ, without being shackled within the *systems* of the ancient Greek philosophical schools. They found this Greek approach appropriate and applicable to their own experience of the life in Christ.

---

[139] For introductory reading see A. Keselopoulos, *Passions and Virtues*, pp. 166-177 and T. Spidlik, *The Spirituality of the Christian East*, Kalamazoo, 1986, pp. 270-281.

For the Fathers of the Church, the knowledge they pursued was not, and never could be, limited to discursive analytical reasoning. Knowledge of God is experiential participation in the life in Christ through ascetic purification, prayerful contemplation, and mystical illumination stemming from, and centered in, the sacramental and liturgical life of the Church.

The patristic experience of knowledge of God is a charisma, or gift, of the Holy Spirit granted to those who are progressing in the Church's therapeutic process of purification, illumination, and theosis:

> Byzantine theology uncovers the ... vision of man, called to 'know' God, to 'participate' in His life, to be 'saved', not simply through ... the rational cognition of prepositional truths, but by 'becoming God'. And this *theosis* of man is radically different in Byzantine theology from the Neoplatonic return to an impersonal One: it is a new expression of the neotestamental life 'in Christ' and in the 'communion of the Holy Spirit.'[140]

The Fathers thus adopted Greek ways of 'knowing' from some of the ancient philosophical traditions and adapted them in the light of Christ.

The point Florovsky is trying to convey when he asserts that to be patristic is to be 'Greek', is that when the Christian Hellenism of the Fathers is neglected, then the entire patristic perspective is also missing.

---

[140] J. Meyendorff, *Byzantine Theology*, p. 3.

Not only is the contemplative, mystical, and ascetical approach to theology lost, which he considers the "best and most valuable part of Byzantine tradition,"[141] but the direct and intimate knowledge of both the positive potential and the negative influences inherent in the Greek philosophical tradition is also lacking.

Florovsky writes, "Russian theological thought did not suffer from Greek dominance, but precisely from a careless and hasty break with Hellenic and Byzantine traditions and ties. This falling out from tradition long left the Russian soul spellbound and barren, for creativity is impossible outside of living traditions."[142]

We too must be true to our apostolic and patristic sources if we want to keep ourselves free and refrain from falling back into a 'western captivity'. If we do not learn from the lessons of history, we too will suffer the same estrangement from patristic tradition that infected Orthodox theological thought in both Greece and Russia in previous centuries.

If such a calamity could happen in these historic Orthodox countries, imagine the damage that would be incurred here in America, where we are already battling the influx of a host of non-Orthodox influences—from Protestantism and Roman Catholicism to the ever-rising threat of secularism. We too must be true to our own apostolic and patristic sources if we want to remain free from outside influences. This is one of the foremost responsibilities of Orthodox students of theology today —to keep the flame of our Fathers alive:

---

[141] G. Florovsky, *The Ways of Russian Theology*, vol. 1, p. 27.
[142] Ibid., vol. 2, p. 300.

The Apostolic preaching is kept alive in the Church, not only merely preserved. In this sense, the teaching of the Fathers is a permanent category of Christian existence, a constant and ultimate measure and criterion of right faith. ... 'The mind of the Fathers' is an intrinsic term of reference in Orthodox theology, no less than the word of Holy Scripture, and indeed never separated from it. ... '*To follow*' the Fathers does *not* mean just '*to quote*' them. 'To follow' the Fathers means to acquire their 'mind', their *phronema*.[143]

We are called not simply to *preserve* patristic tradition. We are called to *pursue* it and to *participate* in it ourselves. From out of the well-spring of Holy Tradition and through our participation in the liturgical life of the Church; by attempting to acquire some share in the Fathers' spirit of humility and life of prayer; by pursuing their path toward purification, illumination, and theosis, students of Orthodox theology are called, and must be committed to, acquiring this same 'mind of the Fathers', which is nothing less than the 'mind of Christ' Himself.[144]

---

[143] G. Florovsky, *Bible, Church and Tradition*, pp. 107-109. Here Fr. Florovsky is using the Greek word φρόνημα, which in addition to 'mind' can also be translated as 'thought', 'purpose', or 'will'; see *A Patristic Greek Lexicon*, p. 1490.
[144] See 1 Cor. 2. 16.

This not only keeps outside influences from infiltrating our inheritance; it also inspires and emboldens us as we confront, address, and reach out to the non-Orthodox around us. Only then can we speak with the same voice as our Fathers—from out of the depths of their same experience, utilizing their same categories of thought, and rightly applying their same method and manner of approach.

The Fathers rarely, if ever, convey their own private opinions or individual ideas. Rather, they speak with conviction from out of the Church's 'catholic consciousness': "Those who ... have received the gift to express this catholic consciousness of the Church, we call them Fathers ... since what they make us hear is not only *their* thought or *their* personal conviction, but moreover the very witness of the Church, for they speak from the depth of its catholic fullness."[145]

This is precisely our task as students of Orthodox theology today: *not* to attempt to convey *our own* personal opinions and ideas, but to always be mindful of the fact that we are called to express the 'catholic' consciousness of the *Church*. We must continue on this patristic way and maintain the mind of our Fathers in order to advance onward into the future. This is the only sure way that we will be able to face any and all of the unforeseen issues, problems, and circumstances that await us tomorrow—always under the guidance of the Holy Spirit: "When the Spirit of truth comes, he will guide you into all the truth."[146]

---

[145] G. Florovsky, *Aspects of Church History*, p. 192. Cf. *Creation and Redemption*, p. 40 [emphasis mine].
[146] John 16. 13 (RSV).

The Proper Balance

The awesome responsibility resting upon the shoulders of students of Orthodox theology cannot be over-emphasized. Our Church Fathers have not provided us with a comprehensive theological manual whereby we can simply look up a particular problem and find easy and neatly prepared solutions.

Some of the theological issues facing us today, such as in the field of bioethics and other medically related issues impacted by ongoing advances in technology, were obviously not addressed by our Church Fathers. Our Church faces circumstances today that did not exist in the past.

How are we to confront these issues? How are we to find solutions to these problems? To what extent are students of Orthodox theology actually allowed or expected to exercise any creativity, freedom, or originality in their work?

The ideal is to find the proper balance between the freedom of academia and faithfulness to our Holy Tradition: "What is wanted, is not to translate the old dogmatic formulas into a modern language, but, on the contrary, to return creatively to the 'ancient' experience, to re-live it in the depth of our being, and to incorporate our thought in the continuous fabric of ecclesial fullness."[147] A proper balance must be found between the elements of creative freedom and faithfulness to ecclesial experience.

---

[147] G. Florovsky, *Aspects of Church History*, p. 197.

While the student of Orthodox theology is free to find skilled and effective ways of expounding, upholding, and expressing the life of the Church, he must be conscious of his responsibility not to exceed the parameters set out by Holy Tradition. The element of freedom can easily lead to a distortion of our theology, whereby it no longer is a service to the Church:

> Personal theological reflection must be animated not by the desire for originality at any price, but by the need to explain what constitutes a common inheritance and ministers to the salvation of the Church's faithful in that age. It must remain intimately bound to the Church's life of prayer and service so that it may deepen and renew that service. Where this is not the case, service in the Church can become a matter of form only, and theology something cold and individualistic.[148]

Freedom of expression and interpretation must not drift off and digress in directions that would pervert the teachings of the Orthodox Faith. It must have its limits. The boundaries set by Holy Tradition must be upheld and never transgressed. Academic freedom can be abused in the name of theological science and can actually lead one, and others, away from the true Faith.

---

[148] D. Staniloae, *The Experience of God*, p. 86. Cf. P. Nellas, *Deification in Christ*, Crestwood, 1987, pp. 102-104.

In order to find the proper harmony between academic freedom and faithfulness to Holy Tradition, we, as students of theology, must uphold our inherent responsibility of preserving the Faith of our Fathers, and unite this in a balanced way with a creative approach to academic pursuits. This balance must always be founded and focused upon our participation in the Church's ascetic, sacramental and liturgical life of prayer, and always in pursuit of the purification of our passions.

Concluding Remarks

To summarize, we have discussed how Orthodox theology considers dogmas as the expression of the life of the Church and how there is a direct link between Orthodox dogma and Orthodox spiritual life. Dogmas are boundaries that separate truth from error. Dogmas protect and preserve the truth of the Church's therapeutic method of purification, illumination and theosis.

We mentioned how the Church officially formulated her dogmas as a result of the need to counter heretical teachings. The Church did not formulate her dogmas for the sake of mere philosophical speculation, nor did the Fathers engage in theological discourse out of curiosity for abstract theoretical propositions.

Rather, the Church was motivated by her concern to protect her faithful by defending her beliefs and practices against heretical teachings, and thus to safeguard her apostolic experience of salvation and sanctification in the glorified and risen Christ.

The importance of experience in relation to the Church's formulation of dogma was also pointed out. It was stressed how dogma presupposes experience, how dogmas express the living experience of the Church, and how only in the *experience* of the life in Christ do dogmas come alive. Dogmas do not displace experience; they only seek to express it.

The danger of systematization was highlighted. The study of dogmatic theology for purposes of academic science alone falls outside the scope of an Orthodox perspective. Theology must be pursued *together* with the *experience* of living faith. It was emphasized that dogmatic theology is not concerned with the systematic study of abstract theoretical definitions, but rather with first *living*, and only then with *expressing*, the Church's experience of her mystical life in Christ.

It was pointed out how the various branches of dogmatic theology are all intimately and intricately integrated and intertwined. Such a holistic perspective, springing forth from the ethos of ecclesial experience and the liturgical life in Christ, is the proper patristic path for pursuing the study of dogma.

We discussed the crucial importance of adhering to our patristic tradition, and how students of Orthodox theology must strive to acquire the mind of the Fathers, and how we must be true to our apostolic and patristic sources. Finally, we mentioned how students of today are called not simply to preserve patristic tradition, but to pursue it and to participate in it ourselves. Students of Orthodox theology are called to acquire the same 'mind of the Fathers'.

Only then will we speak with the same voice as our Fathers, from out of the depths of their same experience, utilizing their same categories of thought, and rightly applying their same method and manner of approach.

The dogmas of the Orthodox Church are truly life-giving medicines. They lead to the cure of our spiritual sickness. They provide the proper therapy for the healing of our fallen soul. They point the way toward the abundant life in Christ.

Such is the Orthodox approach to the study of dogmatic theology.

Chapter Four

THE ORTHODOX ICON: THEOLOGY INCARNATE

Preliminary Remarks

Throughout the history of Eastern Christianity, the icon has always held a preeminent position within the liturgical life, and indeed the entire ethos, of the Orthodox Church. This chapter explains the theology of the icon within the historical context of those who sought to condemn it, as well as of those who fought to defend it.

For many, it is the icon which is the most distinctive feature of the Orthodox Church. Many times it is the vast variety of those warm and tender faces gazing out intently from the countless icons which fill the walls of every Orthodox Church, that offer the initial greeting to any first-time visitor who ventures inside. One's first impressions of Orthodoxy, as well as one's initial inquiries, are often related to the icon.

Yet the reality is that even many Orthodox believers find it difficult to offer a proper reply to the questions: What are icons? Why do you have them? What do they do? Every Orthodox believer would agree that icons are essential to his faith and that icons and Orthodoxy are somehow intimately integrated. While most Orthodox homes hold a host of icons, with some having a special icon corner as the focus of the family's spiritual life, still many Orthodox Christians retain a vague and inadequate understanding of the theological and spiritual truths embodied in the Orthodox icon.

The Theology of the Icon: An Introduction

It is interesting to note, that of the various teachings defended by the Seven Ecumenical Councils in the history of the ancient Eastern Church, only one teaching is upheld as the triumph of Orthodoxy. For example, while the Church's belief in the complete and perfect divinity of the Son of God was defended at the First Ecumenical Council in the year 325, and while the belief in the complete and perfect divinity of the Holy Spirit was upheld at the Second Ecumenical Council of 381, it is only the Church's belief in the veneration of her icons, which was defended at the Seventh Ecumenical Council held in 787, which is proclaimed as the 'Triumph of Orthodoxy'. This defeat of iconoclasm, which sought to destroy the icons and condemn their veneration, is considered as the ultimate 'Triumph' of the Orthodox faith over the ancient heresies of the early Christian Church.

Furthermore, from a liturgical perspective, it is also celebrated, significantly enough, on the very first Sunday of Great Lent. One might rightfully wonder, with the many different and diverse doctrines defended by the ancient Church, why is it that the veneration of icons should merit such a prominent place in both the theology and the liturgical life of the Church?

The answer lies in the fact that it is the icon that incarnates the entire theological tradition of the Orthodox Church. Icons are not simply religious paintings. They are more than an ancient form of Eastern Christian art. They are more than merely pedagogical tools for teaching the tenets of the Faith. For the Orthodox, icons embody the Church's experience of her theology.

Orthodox theology is not concerned with abstract theory; its ultimate concern is spiritual reality. The Church lives her theology. She expresses her experience of divine life through the means of ordinary items from daily life, such as paint and wood. She sets these apart and she blesses them. She sanctifies them and they become holy. The Church takes ordinary paint and wood and transforms them into holy icons.

Essentially, icons are instruments by which the faithful participate in the divine life they believe in. Icons are conduits through which one experiences holiness. They are vehicles that transport the believer toward the eternal. They transcend time and space. They make the eternal present here today. Icons reflect the sensibility of the Orthodox understanding of salvation and sanctification. Indeed, they reflect the 'sensuality' of the Orthodox way of worship.

In this sense St. John Damascene, one of the greatest defenders of the veneration of icons, wrote with regard to the way that the Orthodox worship Christ:

> We use all our senses to produce worthy images of Him, and we sanctify the noblest of the senses, which is that of sight. For just as words edify the ear, so also the image stimulates the eye. What the book is to the literate, the image is to the illiterate. Just as words speak to the ear, so the image speaks to the sight; it brings us understanding. ... through [images people are] led to remember the wonders of old and to worship God, the worker of wonders.[149]

According to the Orthodox faith, the teachings and traditions one upholds and believes in will necessarily influence and inform one's spiritual orientation and the way one worships. And conversely, the way one worships and the objects one reveres and venerates will automatically reveal the theological teachings and the spiritual beliefs by which one lives. To put it more simply, doctrine determines devotion, whereas one's devotion expresses the doctrines he believes in.[150] This is especially true with regard to the Orthodox icon.

---

[149] St. John Damascene, *On the Divine Images* 1. 17, trans. D. Anderson, Crestwood, 1980, pp. 25-26; PG 94, 1248CD.
[150] See G. Florovsky, "Piety must always be guided and checked by dogma." *Creation and Redemption*, p. 173. Cf. V. Lossky, *In the Image and Likeness of God*, p. 196. See p. 51 above.

However, before discussing its historical and spiritual significance, it would be helpful to first try to define and describe what the word 'icon' actually means.

Icon as Image

The Oxford English Dictionary defines the word 'icon', in a general sense, as an 'image' or 'likeness', a 'similitude' or 'semblance'. In reference more specifically to Eastern Orthodoxy, it further defines 'icon' as: "a representation of some sacred personage in painting ... itself regarded as sacred, and honored with relative worship and adoration."[151]

Our English word 'icon' comes from the Greek word 'εἰκών' which also means 'image' or 'likeness', but can also take on the meaning of 'personal description', 'living image' or 'representation', among many other meanings with various nuances.[152]

St. John Damascene also defines image as "a likeness, or a model, or a figure of something, showing in itself what it depicts. An image is not always like its prototype in every way. For the image is one thing, and the thing depicted is another."[153]

In Scripture, we meet the word 'image' or 'εἰκών' for the first time in the Book of Genesis, at the verse where God says, "Let Us make man in Our image, according to Our likeness."[154]

---

[151] *The Oxford English Dictionary*, vol. 1, Oxford, 1971, p. 1366.
[152] *Greek-English Lexicon*, ed. Liddell and Scott, p. 485.
[153] St. John Damascene, *On the Divine Images* 3. 16, pp. 73-74; PG 94, 1337AB.
[154] Gen. 1. 26.

In the ancient Greek translation of the Old Testament, known as the Septuagint, the Greek rendering for the phrase, "in the image and likeness" is "κατ' εἰκόνα καὶ καθ' ὁμοίωσιν."

One would more accurately translate κατ' εἰκόνα as "*according* to the image" and καθ' ὁμοίωσιν as "*according* to the likeness" since 'according to' (κατά) more clearly conveys the idea of *relatedness* to a prototype while still retaining a clear sense of *distinctiveness* as a created being.[155] In the Orthodox perspective, man himself may thus be seen as an 'icon' of God, since he is created 'according to His image' or more literally, according to the 'icon' of God.

In the New Testament, the Greek word 'εἰκών' is used with reference to Christ, the Son of God. In Paul's Letter to the Colossians, he refers to Christ as "the *image* of the invisible God."[156] And of course, in the original Greek, the word he uses for 'image' is 'εἰκών'. So in this sense too, Christ, the Son of God, is literally the 'icon' of the Father.[157]

However, our Orthodox Church Fathers make an important theological distinction here. While man is created *according* to the divine image or *according* to the image of God, Christ—as the Son of God by nature—is considered as *the* image, the *natural* image of God the Father.[158] There is a fundamental difference here.

---

[155] Cf. *Greek-English Lexicon*, p. 883.
[156] Col. 1. 15. See also 2 Cor. 4. 4.
[157] Cf. John 1. 18 and Heb. 1. 3.
[158] Cf. John 14. 9, "He who has seen Me has seen the Father."

St. John Damascene explains, "There are different kinds of images. First there is the natural image. ... The Son is the natural image of the Father, precisely similar to the Father in every way, except that He is begotten by the Father [that is to say, He is the only-begotten Son of the Father] ... Therefore the first kind of image is the natural image."[159]

He goes on further to describe another kind of image, an image that God *creates* as an imitation of Himself, that is to say, man (or mankind).[160] This pertains to man as being created according to the image of God. So we see then that Christ is the image of God by *nature*, whereas man is created *according* to the divine image. Or to put it another way, Christ is the *natural* image of God, while man is a *created* image. Christ is *the* image of God, according to *whose* image man is created.[161]

In Orthodox anthropology, mankind is created to participate in the divine life of God. This is the essential meaning of the Scriptural account of the creation of man, "Then God said, 'Let Us make man in Our image, according to Our likeness ... So God created man in His own image; in the image of God He created him ..."[162]

---

[159] St. John Damascene, *On the Divine Images* 3. 18, pp. 74-75; PG 94, 1337C-1340B.

[160] "[Another] kind of image is made by God as an imitation of Himself: namely, man. How can what is created share the nature of Him who is uncreated, except by imitation. ... For God says, 'Let us make man according to our own image and likeness." Ibid. 3. 20, p. 76; PG 94, 1340CD.

[161] For further reading on man as created in the image of Christ, see P. Nellas, *Deification in Christ*, Crestwood, 1987, pp. 21-42.

[162] Gen. l. 26, 27.

This passage conveys the fundamental truth that man is a spiritual being, created *in*, or *according to*, the image of God, and that the true meaning of human existence is understood only in its proper theological perspective. Apart from this, man becomes something he was not originally created to be.

The Orthodox Church Fathers teach that when man distances himself from his Creator, he restricts himself to a life separated from God. He then not only forfeits his sanctification as an icon created according to the image of God, but he also fails to comprehend the fundamental purpose of his existence. Communion with God and participation in the life of divine grace constitute man's natural element. It is the presence of the divine image according to which he is created, and it is his potential for divine likeness toward which he is called, that distinguish man from the animal kingdom.

Man is thus created and called to grow, as an icon in the divine *image*, into the fullness of divine *likeness*. Although he has fallen from his original splendor, and in spite of the fact that he is now born into a fallen state; into a world of sickness and suffering; into a world of dysfunction and death—still, man retains the image of God in which he was initially created.

According to the Orthodox Church, the image of God in fallen man is certainly distorted and disfigured, but it has not been entirely annihilated or completely destroyed. Furthermore, the goal of Orthodox spiritual life is not simply to restore the 'image of God', to restore that 'icon' of God according to which man was originally created. Even more than that, it is to attain to the 'likeness of God' in Christ.

The exact meaning of the phrase 'in the image and likeness' has occupied the minds of many Christian writers throughout the history of the Church. For Orthodox anthropology, the term 'image' has a different meaning from the term 'likeness'. 'Image' may be seen as the potential inherent in man for sanctification, while 'likeness' refers to its perfection. Or in other words, one could say 'image' implies 'potentiality', whereas 'likeness' implies 'actuality'.[163]

Man was not originally created in a state of completed perfection. He was, however, endowed with the unique freedom to *choose*, to either live in pursuit of achieving his full potential, or else to digress toward the desecration and defacement of his true dignity as an icon of God. Only through the proper use of his God-given freedom can man cooperate with divine grace in restoring the image of God within him, and attain to divine likeness, for which he was originally created.[164]

---

[163] Refer to Elder Sophrony, "When it is God's good pleasure to unite with the human being, man perceives within himself the action of a Divine force which transfigures him and makes him no longer just potentially godlike—in the image of God—but actually godlike in likeness of being." *Saint Silouan the Athonite*, p. 184. Prof. Georgios Mantzaridis comments further, "Likeness to God, while it constitutes the goal of human existence, is not imposed on man, but is left to his own free will. By submitting himself freely to God's will and being constantly guided by His grace, man can cultivate and develop the gift of the 'image'..." *The Deification of Man*, trans. L. Sherrard, Crestwood, 1984, p. 22.

[164] In the teaching of St. Irenaeus of Lyons, man is presented created as a 'child', who must grow into the full maturity of manhood. See St. Irenaeus of Lyons, *Demonstration of the Apostolic Preaching* 12; Sources Chrétiennes, vol. 62, ed. L. M. Froidevaux, Paris, 1959, pp. 50-51.

In Orthodox tradition, the attainment of divine likeness is referred to as *theosis* or *deification*. These two terms are synonymous and they refer to the sanctification of human nature. All human beings are called to grow and progress continually by divine grace into the likeness of God. According to Orthodox teaching, God grants to man *through grace* that which is His *by nature*, that is, divine life and likeness. This is the teaching of the Apostle Peter, "Be partakers of divine nature..."[165] and elsewhere, "But as He who called you is holy, you also be holy in all your conduct, because it is written, 'Be holy, for I am holy'."[166] God grants to man *through grace* that which is His *by nature*, that is to say, His divine life. Man was created to be a vessel of divine life, an icon of divine likeness.

This ancient and apostolic teaching on man's participation in divine life and growth into divine likeness, or deification, has important spiritual ramifications. In fact, the whole debate between those who tried to condemn icons and those who died to defend them, centered on the correct understanding of the Orthodox Church's experience of salvation and sanctification in Christ. The whole debate over the propriety of the veneration of holy icons was actually a debate over the proper understanding of salvation and sanctification in Christ.

---

[165] 2 Peter 1. 4.
[166] 1 Peter 1. 15,16.

In reality, the iconoclastic controversy was an extension of the disputes concerning the correct understanding of Christ.[167] It was a *Christ*-centered controversy, just as the icon is a Christ-centered phenomenon.

Terminology: Iconophile and Iconoclast

Having familiarized ourselves with this fundamental theological foundation, we move on to a brief overview of the iconoclastic controversy. First, however, it will be helpful to define two important terms.

The first term is 'iconophile', from the Greek 'εἰκονοφίλης' which comes from two words, the first is 'εἰκών' which we have already mentioned, and the second, 'φίλος', which means 'friend' or 'beloved'.[168] The noun ἡ φιλία means love in the sense of 'affectionate regard or friendship'.[169] Interestingly, in modern Greek, the noun 'τό φιλί' means a 'kiss'. So an iconophile is a 'friend of icons', a 'lover of icons', or if we want to go further, we could say an iconophile is one who 'kisses' icons.

This is in direct contrast to our second term, 'iconoclast'. From the Greek word, 'εἰκονοκλάστης' it comes from 'εἰκών', and the verb 'κλάω' which means 'to break' or 'break off'. An iconoclast is one who 'breaks' or destroys icons.

---

[167] Cf. G. Florovsky, 'The Iconoclastic Controversy' in *Christianity and Culture*, Belmont, 1974, p. 103.
[168] *Greek-English Lexicon*, ed. Liddell and Scott, p. 1939. 'Iconophiles' are also referred to as 'iconodules' which means 'servants of icons'.
[169] Ibid., p. 1934.

We are familiar with the word 'iconoclast' as it is used in colloquial English when referring to one who "assails or attacks cherished beliefs ... venerated institutions,"[170] or established conventions. Iconophiles, therefore, are friends of icons who kiss them. Iconoclasts are rebels who attack them.

Iconclasm: A Brief Overview—Phase One

Within the annals of Byzantine history, the iconoclastic controversy is considered more than a dispute over the use of icons in liturgical worship. In reality it was a theological heresy which rejected the sanctity of icons and condemned their veneration. It lasted, for the most part, well over a hundred years, from 726 to 843.

It was basically a battle between a few iconoclastic emperors together with the majority of the imperial army, who were lined up against the vast array of Orthodox monks, who had the support and sympathy of countless clergy and the multitude of lay people.

Iconoclasm was promoted by the imperial powers. While it was two Byzantine *Emperors* who originally initiated the persecution, it was two Byzantine *Empresses* who instigated its final defeat.

The controversy was mainly concentrated within the imperial capital of Constantinople. Although the persecutions of iconophiles did extend out into the provinces, they were less consistent and less harsh than

---

[170] *The Oxford English Dictionary*, vol. 1, p. 1367.

the more thorough and rigorous persecutions, in some cases even martyrdom, which took place within the walls of Constantinople.[171]

In the early eighth century there were a few isolated cases of those who spoke out against the veneration of icons, citing the Old Testament commandment against the worship of any graven image.[172] However, iconoclasm officially became an outright controversy in the year 726 when the Byzantine Emperor Leo III commanded that a prominent icon of Christ be taken down from the main entrance of the imperial palace. Reaction was immediate and violent. A riot quickly ensued; but this only hardened the emperor's heart even further.

In the year 730 Leo deposed the Orthodox Patriarch and issued an imperial decree declaring all icons as idols and demanding their immediate destruction. He initiated the first persecution against iconophiles, especially against the monasteries, since it was the monks who were the most fervent advocates of the veneration of icons.[173] During this period, Leo's activities were restricted to destroying icons, defacing ecclesiastical decoration, and desecrating other holy artifacts. At this point there is no verifiable proof of any actual martyrdom.[174]

---

[171] *The Oxford Dictionary of Byzantium*, vol. 2, Oxford, 1991, p. 975.
[172] See ibid. Cf. Ex. 20. 2. 4-5.
[173] See *The Oxford Dictionary of the Christian Church*, p. 815.
[174] See *The Oxford Dictionary of Byzantium*, vol. 2, p. 975.

However, things were about to change. When Leo III died in the year 741, his son Constantine V ascended to the imperial throne.[175] Constantine embarked on an even more rigorous iconoclastic crusade than his father before him. He called together a local council in the year 754, which for the first time brought a theological perspective to the iconoclastic position. The new emperor himself wrote treatises promoting iconoclasm. Basically, his claim was that since Christ is truly God, it is heretical to portray or attempt to depict Him.[176]

The council issued an official decree proclaiming all icons as idols, including those of the saints. It declared that all icons must be destroyed. Significantly, none of the other Eastern Orthodox patriarchates, such as the Churches of Alexandria, Antioch or Jerusalem, nor even the Bishop of Rome, were invited to attend this council.

Armed with his decree, Constantine V set out to eradicate the Orthodox icon: "On his orders, the churches were despoiled, sacred vessels adorned with icons were desecrated, frescoes were whitewashed over, holy images on wood were burnt. Only paintings of secular subjects were allowed, and the Cross alone

---

[175] "Byzantine sources displayed their hostility toward [Constantine V] by nicknaming him ... 'Copronymus' (dung-named) for supposedly having defecated while being baptized." *The Oxford Dictionary of Byzantium*, vol. 1, Oxford, 1991, p. 501.

[176] The iconoclast Christological argument was basically that any pictorial depiction of Christ would lead to either a confusion concerning the unity of the perfect divinity and complete humanity of Christ, or it would lead to a separation of His two natures. For further reading see G. Florovsky, 'The Iconoclastic Controversy' in *Christianity and Culture*, pp. 107-115.

was accepted as worthy of veneration. All who opposed this policy were severely punished, especially the monks. [They were] harassed, exiled and tortured."[177]

The persecutions progressively intensified, especially among those iconophiles within the ranks of the army, the church leadership and the government. In particular, the assault against the monks turned into an anti-monastic movement.[178] The persecutions became more violent and brutal. Even among the clergy, some began to relent.

At this point, in the decade of the 760's, many Orthodox monks became martyrs in defense of the holy icons.[179] We read the following account from the life of St. Stephen the New, who was one of the greatest martyrs who died in defense of the veneration of icons: "Then they began a methodical persecution of monks, less deferential than bishops to imperial authority, and always ready to resist Emperors who fell away from the faith. The monasteries were closed; some were used as barracks, [others] as public baths, or for other purposes. The monks were subjected to insults and risked torture unless they would dress as laymen and [even] marry. Those who refused were mutilated, or brutally treated in other ways, before being sent into exile."[180]

---

[177] *The Synaxarion*, vol. 2, November 28th, St. Stephen the New, ed. Hieromonk Macarios, trans. C. Hookway, Ormylia, 1999, p. 266.
[178] See *The Oxford Dictionary of Byzantium*, vol. 1, p. 501.
[179] See *The Oxford Dictionary of the Christian Church*, p. 815.
[180] *The Synaxarion*, vol. 2, op. cit., pp. 266-267.

St. Stephen was eventually arrested in Constantinople and imprisoned with over 300 other monks:

> All bore in their bodies the marks of their glorious combats: some had suffered the loss of their noses, their ears or their tongues, others had been shamefully treated and covered in filth. ... After eleven months of imprisonment ... the notice of the death-sentence pronounced on [Stephen], the leader of the Orthodox party, had been posted up [all over the City], in order to frighten people who were concealing monks or confessors of the faith in their homes. In the commotion that followed, the mob, roused up by the soldiers, broke open the [prison], seized the Saint and dragged him through the streets of Constantinople, showering him with blows and insults. ... [An unidentified assailant] hit him on the head with a wooden beam, breaking open his skull ... The corpse of the Saint was then dreadfully mutilated and thrown into [a] ... ditch ... This happened on November 28th, [the year] 766.[181]

Such was the brutality of the Emperor's persecution. Constantine V finally died in 775. He was succeeded by his son Leo IV. Although Leo favored iconoclasm, the persecutions actually declined during his short reign.[182]

---

[181] Ibid.

[182] "Leo supported iconoclasm but actively persecuted iconophiles only in August, 780, when he had a number of court officials

He died after only five years as emperor, in the year 780. Upon his death, his wife the Empress Irene ruled as regent for their nine-year old son.[183] Irene was a devoted iconophile. In spite of the iconoclastic inclinations of the army, she did all she could to overturn the previous policies of persecution.[184] She was able to engineer the election of an iconophile as Patriarch of Constantinople and with his support the Seventh Ecumenical Council was held in the year 787, which decreed the restoration of the veneration of holy icons.

The Distinction between Worship and Veneration

The doctrinal statement of the Seventh Ecumenical Council carefully distinguishes between two very important theological terms. The first term is *worship*, which is due to God alone. The second term is *veneration*, which is offered to the saints.[185] In Greek, the word for worship is λατρεία (*latreia*), whereas the word for veneration is προσκύνησις (*proskynesis*).

---

beaten, tortured and imprisoned." *The Oxford Dictionary of Byzantium*, vol. 2, p. 1209.

[183] Their son was Constantine VI. Seventeen years later, "In 797 she dethroned ... Constantine, thus becoming the first female Byzantine autocrat, but was herself toppled by Nikephoros I in 802 and exiled to Lesbos." Ibid., p. 1008.

[184] See *The Oxford Dictionary of the Christian Church*, p. 815.

[185] See *Creeds and Confessions of Faith in the Christian Tradition*, vol. 1, ed. J. Pelikan and V. Hotchkiss, New Haven, 2003, p. 237.

This crucial distinction between 'worship' and 'veneration' lies at the very heart of the Orthodox position. The Church was quite precise when she spelled out her teaching. It is God alone Who is worthy of *worship* and adoration; whereas the saints and their icons are only to be *venerated* and honored.

St. John Damascene explains, "Let us understand that there are different degrees of worship. First of all there is [worship] or adoration, which we offer to God, who alone by nature is worthy to be *worshipped*. Then, for the sake of Him ... we [venerate] or *honor* His friends and companions ..."[186]

It is clear then, that Orthodox Christians only worship their one God the Holy Trinity: the Father, the Son—Who they believe became man in Jesus Christ, and the Holy Spirit. On the other hand, they certainly venerate the saints and they venerate their holy icons.

The Orthodox *worship* Christ, Who they believe is God by nature; yet they *venerate* Orthodox saints, who being created according to the image of God, have attained to the likeness of God by grace. And they venerate Orthodox icons, which in turn are created according to the image of whom they represent.

Another important point to be made is that the veneration and honor offered to the icon is not limited to the image itself. The honor passes on to the prototype of the image, to the saint himself.

---

[186] St. John Damascene, *On the Divine Images* 1. 14, p. 21; PG 94, 1244AB. Cf. ibid., 1. 6, 1. 8, and 3. 27-39, pp. 17, 18 and 82-88, respectively; PG 94, 1237B, 1237CD-1239AB, 1348D-1356B.

The decree of the Seventh Ecumenical Council plainly teaches, "The honor paid to an image traverses it, reaching the model, and he who venerates the image, venerates the person represented in that image."[187]

Icons are thus conduits that convey the veneration and honor offered by the Church to the prototype depicted therein. The Church had already clarified this teaching, as early as the fourth century, as we see in the writings of St. Basil the Great: "The honor given [to] the image passes to the prototype."[188]

Thus, the Orthodox Church teaches that the veneration or honor offered to an icon passes on to its prototype, the saint himself. And the honor bestowed to the saint is thereby ultimately passed on to his or her prototype, Who is Christ—according to Whose *image* all mankind is created, and according to Whose *likeness* all saints have become: "Inasmuch as every Saint of the Church reflects, as it were, the light of Christ Himself, the Prototype of every icon is Christ Himself, Who is '*the* Icon of the invisible God (Col. 1. 15). ... Or to put it more simply, according to Orthodox theology, every icon is an icon of Christ, the real and momentous presence of God in [the] midst of mankind, the God Who is with us, Emmanuel (cf. Matt. 1. 23)."[189]

---

[187] *Creeds and Confessions of Faith in the Christian Tradition*, vol. 1, pp. 237-239. Cf. G. Florovsky, 'The Iconoclastic Controversy' in *Christianity and Culture*, pp. 116-117.
[188] St. Basil the Great, *On the Holy Spirit* 18. 45, trans. D. Anderson, Crestwood, 1980, p. 72; PG 32, 149C.
[189] Encyclical of SCOBA for the Sunday of Orthodoxy, March 16, 2008, p. 2.

Iconoclasm: A Brief Overview—Phase Two

With the conclusion of the Seventh Ecumenical Council in 787 and the proclamation of the imperial decree reinstating the veneration of holy icons, the first phase of the iconoclastic controversy came to a close. However, there was a second and shorter phase, lasting from 814 to 843. Iconoclasm had remained a potent force among the army. Two emperors in particular, Leo V who ruled from 813-820 and Theophilos who ruled from 829-842 again revived the persecutions. When Theophilos died, his wife the Empress Theodora became regent for their four year old son.

Much like St. Irene, the Empress St. Theodora was also an ardent iconophile. She quickly set out to restore the veneration of icons and recalled those who had been exiled by her husband. With the aid of an eminent adviser within the imperial court, Theoktistos, she was able to have an iconophile, Methodios, appointed as Patriarch of Constantinople.

On March 11, 843, the first Sunday of Great Lent, all three of them, the Empress Theodora, the Patriarch Methodios and the powerful imperial advisor Theoktistos, organized a widely popular festival commemorating the definitive Triumph of Orthodoxy, which included a royal and symbolic procession of holy icons along the streets of Constantinople, from the Church of the Theotokos to the Great Church of Hagia Sophia.[190]

---

[190] See J. McGuckin, *Patristic Theology*, Louisville, 2004, p. 177.

There, in Hagia Sophia, a divine liturgy was celebrated in honor of the restoration of the veneration of the holy icons and the final defeat of iconoclasm. This event further served to disperse even those dissenting elements within the military, who had retained their iconoclastic leanings.[191] Thus the iconoclastic controversy quickly came to a close.

Soon afterward, before the beginning of the tenth century, an annual commemoration marking the restoration of icons was introduced into the Orthodox liturgical year.[192] From that time forward, on the first Sunday of Great Lent, the Church has always celebrated the 'Triumph of Orthodoxy'. This annual celebration includes a procession of icons and the reading of the anathemas against all the major heresies throughout the history of the Church, concluding with the condemnation of iconoclasm. Such was the end of the heresy that sought to eradicate the Orthodox icon from the face of the Eastern Church.

Byzantine historians are not in total agreement as to the actual contributing factors motivating the iconoclastic movement.[193] Some claim economic factors, wherein the emperors sought to exploit iconoclastic ideology in order to take over wealthy church properties, particularly those of the landed monasteries.

---

[191] See ibid.
[192] See *The Oxford Dictionary of Byzantium*, vol. 3, Oxford, 1991, p. 2122.
[193] See G. Florovsky, 'The Iconoclastic Controversy' in *Christianity and Culture*, pp. 101-110.

Others consider iconoclasm as an attempt on behalf of the emperors to institute imperial authority over Church affairs.[194] Others claim iconoclasm may have been initiated in order to facilitate the conversion of Muslims and Jews, who would have considered the veneration of icons as a hindrance to accepting the faith.

Regardless of the potential political motivations, the underlying issue remained one of theology and spirituality. It was ultimately a question of the meaning of salvation and the sanctification of created nature in Christ. The iconoclastic understanding and experience of Christ was obviously at odds with that of the Orthodox Church.

Icon and Incarnation

The Orthodox Church teaches that man is called to participate in divine nature. Man is called to a union and communion with God. Such a union is made possible only by virtue of the Incarnation, wherein God and human nature have been forever united in the Person of Christ. And not only *human* nature but together with it, *all* created nature, also created by the hands of God, has the potential to be sanctified, and to be restored to its original and proper relationship with its Creator. Such is the Orthodox belief in salvation and sanctification.

Such a belief was not shared by the iconoclasts. In fact, in the eyes of the Church, iconoclasm was a condemnation of such beliefs.

---

[194] See *The Oxford Dictionary of Byzantium*, vol. 2, p. 976.

The iconoclasts based their arguments on the Ten Commandments of the Old Testament. In the Book of Exodus, God, in the second commandment forbids the making of any image, "You shall not make for yourself a graven image, or any likeness of anything that is in heaven above, or that is in the earth beneath ..."[195]

However, the Church Fathers point out that it is not the actual making of images that God prohibits, but it is idolatry and the *worship* of such images that He forbids. Even in the same Book of Exodus, God commands Moses to make images of angelic cherubim that were to be placed on the Ark of the Covenant, "And you shall make two cherubim of gold; of hammered work you shall make them at the two ends of the mercy seat. Make one cherub at one end, and the other cherub at the other end."[196]

The Temple of Solomon also contained images of lions, oxen and cherubim.[197] The fact that these man-made images are so closely connected to the Jewish worship of God shows clearly that it was not images themselves that were forbidden. It is their worship as gods which the Lord forbids: "You shall not make for yourselves gods of silver, and gods of gold you shall not make for yourselves,"[198] commands the God of Israel.

---

[195] Ex. 20. 4 (RSV).
[196] Ex. 25. 18-19. See Ex. 26. 31.
[197] See 1 Kings 7. 29 (LXX 3 Kings 7. 16).
[198] Ex. 21. 2 (SAAS). Refer to St. John Damascene where, in an imaginary dialogue with Moses, he asks, "How do you explain this, O Moses? On the one hand you say, 'You shall not make for yourself a graven image, or any likeness', and yet you yourself

A further argument of the iconoclasts was that it is impossible to depict God since He is invisible and formless. Therefore any depiction of Christ, Who the Church believes is God by nature, is blasphemous, since it attempts to depict His divine nature. Since God is invisible, it is impossible to portray Him. God Himself proclaims to Moses, "You cannot see my face; for man shall not see me, and live."[199] Even the Gospel of John asserts, "No one has ever seen God ..."[200]

Certainly before the Incarnation, before God became man, it was in fact impossible to depict Him, and it would have been sacrilegious to do so. But now, in light of the Incarnation of the Son of God, in light of the fact that God has assumed human flesh—that God now has a human body and a human face—the human form of Jesus Christ can definitely be depicted. Not only *can* He be depicted, but for the Orthodox, the Incarnate Son of God *must* be depicted.

---

have cherubim woven on the veil [of the tabernacle] and two cherubim fashioned of pure gold." He then has Moses reply with these words, "I did not say, 'You shall not make images of cherubim, which spread out their wings overshadowing the mercy seat'. What I did say was, 'You shall not make for yourselves molten gods', and, 'You shall not make for yourself any likeness; you shall not bow down to them and serve them as God, nor shall you adore the creature instead of the Creator. You shall have no other gods before Me; you shall adore no creature as God; you shall not adore the creature instead of the Creator'." St. John Damascene, *On the Divine Images* 2. 9, pp. 56-57; PG 94, 1292CD-1293A.
[199] Ex. 33. 20 (RSV).
[200] John 1. 18 (RSV).

According to Orthodox teaching, when the Son of God became man, not only did He remain fully divine and truly God, but He also became fully and truly human. The perfect God became, and still *is*, perfect man. The belief that God became man and took on human flesh, with a human face, and spoke with a human voice, warrants, and indeed *requires* that He now be depicted; that His face be portrayed; that His image be rendered in color and in light.

Through the means of holy icons, the face of Jesus Christ is made present, and His presence becomes tangible within the life of the Orthodox Church. Christ proclaims to His disciples, "Blessed are your eyes for they see, and your ears for they hear; for assuredly, I say to you that many prophets and righteous men desired to see what you see, and did not see it, and to hear what you hear, and did not hear it."[201] Elsewhere Christ declares, "He who has seen Me has seen the Father."[202]

From an Orthodox theological perspective, every icon of the Lord Jesus Christ is a testimony to His Incarnation. Every icon is a declaration of the Church's belief that God has become man. Every icon is a proclamation announcing that God has truly revealed Himself. The Apostle John the Theologian proclaims: "And the Word became flesh and dwelt among us ... we have beheld his glory, glory as of the only Son from the Father."[203]

---

[201] Matt. 13. 16-17.
[202] John 14. 9.
[203] John 1. 14 (RSV).

And yes, the Gospel does assert that "No one has ever seen God;" but immediately following the Evangelist adds, "the only Son ... has made Him *known*."[204] The Orthodox icon is thus a theological statement, an outpouring in color of the Church's belief in the Incarnation of God.

Before concluding, it must be mentioned that the Church does not embrace just any portrayal or depiction of Christ and His saints, nor do artistic skills alone qualify one as an Orthodox iconographer. There is a long history of time-honored Tradition that must be upheld, with definite set patterns and practices sanctioned by the Church. These refer not only to artistic style but also to the spiritual life of the iconographer. Metropolitan Kallistos (Ware) explains:

> Because the icon is a part of Tradition, icon painters are not free to adapt or innovate as they please; for their work must reflect, not their own aesthetic sentiments, but the mind of the Church. Artistic inspiration is not excluded, but it is exercised within certain prescribed rules. It is important that icon painters should be good artists, but it is even more important that they should be sincere Christians, living within the spirit of Tradition, preparing themselves for their work by means of Confession and Holy Communion.[205]

---

[204] John 1. 18 (RSV).
[205] T. Ware, *The Orthodox Church*, London, 1993, p. 206.

Conclusion

The Orthodox icon, in addition to its Christological perspective, also bears witness to the Church's *cosmological* teaching as well. The icon reflects the Orthodox understanding of the inherent goodness of creation. It manifests the Church's faith in the latent sanctity and potential *sacramentality* of created matter; it proclaims the presence of the divine within our created and material world.[206] Leonid Ouspensky explains:

> By denying the human image of God, [iconoclasts] consequently denied the sanctification of matter in general. They disavowed all human holiness and even denied the very possibility of sanctification, [and] the deification of man. In other words, by refusing to accept the consequences of the Incarnation [which include] the sanctification of the visible [and] material world—iconoclasm undermined the entire economy of salvation. ... Through the denial of the image, Christianity became an abstract theory, it became *dis-incarnate,* so to speak.[207]

---

[206] See J. McGuckin, *Patristic Theology*, p. 177.
[207] L. Ouspensky, *Theology of the Icon*, vol. 1, Crestwood, 1992, p. 146 [emphasis mine].

In the eyes of the Orthodox, iconoclasm embodied a belief in the dis-incarnation of God, a dis-engagement of God from His creation; a final divorce of the Creator from His cosmos. The Orthodox Church rejects those teachings which consider created matter and the material world as some kind of an illusion, or as somehow impure.[208] In the words of Metropolitan Kallistos:

> The Iconoclasts, by repudiating all representations of God, failed to take full account of the Incarnation. They fell, as so many puritans have done, into a kind of dualism. Regarding matter as a defilement, they wanted a religion freed from all contact with what is material; for they thought that what is spiritual must be non-material. But this is to betray the Incarnation,

---

[208] In this light, Fr. Florovsky observes: "Matter in general is not something low or despicable, but a creation of God. Ever since the uncontainable [Word] was contained in it, matter has been worthy of praise and veneration. Therefore, material images are not only possible, but also necessary, and have a direct and positive religious significance ... This justifies iconography and the veneration of icons in general ... In the Old Testament human nature was still under censure—death was considered a punishment, and the body of the dead impure. But now everything has been renewed. We have been illumined since the time when God [the Word] became flesh." G. Florovsky, *The Byzantine Fathers of the Sixth to Eighth Centuries*, Vaduz, 1987, p. 283. Elsewhere, Fr. Florovsky links iconoclasm with Origenism, "The defense of Holy Icons was, in some sense, an indirect refutation of Origenism, a new act in the story of the 'Origenistic controversies'." 'The Iconoclastic Controversy' in *Christianity and Culture*, p. 110. For further reading see ibid., pp. 107-115.

by allowing no place to Christ's humanity, to His body; it is to forget that our body as well as our soul must be saved and transfigured. The Iconoclast controversy ... was not merely a controversy about religious art, but about the Incarnation, about human salvation, about the salvation of the entire material cosmos."[209]

We see then why the Orthodox, and the monks in particular, were so determined to defend the Church's veneration of her holy icons. It would have been wrong for them not to do so. It would have been a denial of the Incarnation. It would have been a rejection of their experience of the life in Christ; a rejection of their personal experience of icons in their own spiritual lives.

---

[209] T. Ware, *The Orthodox Church*, p. 33. See N. Matsoukas, 'The Economy of the Holy Spirit', *The Ecumenical Review*, 41. 3, July, 1989, p. 401. See also J. Meyendorff, 'Orthodox Theology Today', *SVTQ*, 13. 1-2, 1969, pp. 82-83. Elder Vasileios adds further, "But the West, too, failed to understand fully the Eastern Church's struggle, it failed to realize what it was all about, and did not take part in it. This is why, seven years after the Seventh Ecumenical Council of 787, Charlemagne, who can be called the father of western culture, called the Council of Frankfurt (794) which condemned the Seventh Council and rejected its teaching." Archim. Vasileios, *The Fayyum Portraits*, Montreal, 2001, pp. 15-16.

We conclude with St. John Damascene:

I do not worship matter; I worship the Creator of matter who became matter for my sake, who willed to take His abode in matter; who worked out my salvation through matter. Never will I cease honoring the matter which wrought my salvation! ... Because of this I salute all remaining matter with reverence, because God has filled it with His grace and power. Through it my salvation has come to me. ... is not the Body and Blood of our Lord matter? Either do away with the honor and veneration these things deserve, or accept the tradition of the Church and the veneration of images. Do not despise matter. God has made nothing despicable.[210]

---

[210] St. John Damascene, *On the Divine Images* 1. 16, pp. 23-24; PG 94, 1245BC. He writes elsewhere, "I do not worship matter; I worship the Creator of matter, who became matter for me, taking up His abode in matter, and accomplishing my salvation through matter. 'And the Word became flesh and dwelt among us'. It is obvious to everyone that flesh is matter, and that it is created. I salute matter and approach it with reverence, and I worship that through which my salvation has come. I honor it, not as God, but because it is full of divine grace and strength." Ibid., 2. 14, pp. 61-62; PG 94, 1300B.

Epilogue

For the Fathers of the Orthodox Church, when one becomes holy by divine grace, his or her sanctification is not limited to his own nature. It extends outward toward the natural environment in which he lives. Indeed the saint embraces the entire cosmos with his, or her, Christ-like love for *all* creation.

In this sense, man is considered as a high priest of God's creation. Through his prayers he calls down the grace of the Holy Spirit, not only for himself, but for all mankind, and for all of creation, restoring matter back to its original purpose and to its proper relationship to both God and man.

No one is saved or sanctified alone. The saints are conscious of their inherent unity with all mankind, and indeed with all of creation. Not only does the Fall of man have cosmic consequences for the entire creation, but man's salvation and sanctification in Christ also have a similar effect.

The Orthodox icon points toward the potential sanctification of all God's creation. In an existential and eschatological way, it proclaims this sanctification as a present, though not yet perfected, reality.

And in a world that has become a global marketplace of idolatry and false idols, such as money and power, celebrity and fame; the light of the icon shines on brightly, illuminating the Orthodox understanding of man's true spiritual potential.

This is what makes the icon so relevant for us Orthodox. This is what makes Orthodoxy so relevant for today. This is why we Orthodox kiss our icons, and offer incense before them, and sprinkle them with holy water. We light candles before them, and pray before them; we cry before them, and bow before them. They are there when we are married, and they are there when we are buried. They are present with us always, from our baptism to our grave.

Many people today tend to identify the Orthodox Church with incense and icons. It is interesting to note, how during the Divine Liturgy, when the priest censes the iconostasis and the other icons in the Church, he also censes the people in the congregation.

The Church does this because she believes that it is man himself who is the greatest icon of all. Man created in the image of God, is indeed a living icon of the living God. The Church censes the icons of paint and wood, as a way to honor them. And she censes the icons of flesh and blood, honoring the image within, venerating the icon inside.[211]

To venerate and honor painted icons is a good thing. Yet it is even better to venerate and honor the living icons of God, who are our fellow human beings.[212] Every man, and every woman, has been created in the image of God, whether we are black or white, Catholic or Protestant, Muslim or Jew.

---

[211] See A. Coniaris, *Introducing the Orthodox Church*, Minneapolis, 1982, p. 177.
[212] See ibid.

If I venerate painted icons, yet disregard and despise God's *living* icons, then I am simply reenacting the iconoclastic heresy. I become like those Byzantine emperors who persecuted divine images. And if I fail to honor the holy icon imprinted within my neighbor, and when I neglect to respect the divine image engraved in each and every human being, I become in fact, the worst kind of iconoclast.

The Orthodox Church believes that all of us are made in the same image and that all of us should strive for the same likeness. All mankind, whether those living on earth or those who have passed away, even those yet to be born, are all united as one.

We all share one and the same human nature. We all belong to one and the same human family—the family of mankind. Every one of us who is born into this world, indeed every member of the Orthodox Church, is a living icon of God.

And what kind of a Church would we be, if only we, as Orthodox Christians, could honor each other, as we do the holy icons, of our Holy Orthodox Church?

Select Bibliography

Patristic Writings

BASIL THE GREAT. *Hexaemeron.* Trans. B. Jackson. The Nicene and Post-Nicene Fathers, 2nd series, vol. 8. Grand Rapids: W. B. Eerdmans, 1989.

——— *On the Holy Spirit.* Trans. D. Anderson. Crestwood: St. Vladimir's Seminary Press, 1980.

DOROTHEOS OF GAZA. *Discourses.* Trans. E. Wheeler. Kalamazoo: Cistercian Publications, 1977.

EVAGRIUS. *Chapters on Prayer.* Trans. J. E. Bamberger. Kalamazoo: Cistercian Publications, 1981.

GREGORY OF NYSSA. *The Life of Moses.* Trans. A. Malherbe and E. Ferguson. The Classics of Western Spirituality. New York: Paulist Press, 1978.

GREGORY PALAMAS. *Defense of the Hesychasts* (under the title *The Triads*). Trans. N. Gendle. The Classics of Western Spirituality. New York: Paulist Press, 1983.

GREGORY THE THEOLOGIAN. *Select Orations.* Trans. C. G. Browne and J. E. Swallow. The Nicene and Post-Nicene Fathers, 2nd series, vol. 7. Grand Rapids: W. B. Eerdmans, 1989.

IRENAEUS OF LYONS. *Against the Heresies: Book I.* Trans. D. J. Unger. Ancient Christian Writers, vol. 55. New York: Paulist Press, 1992.

──── *On the Apostolic Preaching.* Trans. J. Behr. Crestwood: St. Vladimir's Seminary Press, 1997.

ISAAC THE SYRIAN. *The Ascetical Homilies.* Trans. Holy Transfiguration Monastery. Boston: Holy Transfiguration Monastery, 1984.

JOHN CLIMACUS. *The Ladder of Divine Ascent.* Trans. C. Luibheid and N. Russell. The Classics of Western Spirituality. New York: Paulist Press, 1982.

JOHN DAMASCENE. *On the Divine Images.* Trans. D. Anderson. Crestwood: St. Vladimir's Seminary Press, 1980.

SYMEON THE NEW THEOLOGIAN. *Ethical Discourses.* Trans. A. Golitzin. *On the Mystical Life,* vol. 1. Crestwood: St. Vladimir's Seminary Press, 1995.

──── *The Discourses.* Trans. C. J. deCatanzaro. The Classics of Western Spirituality. New York: Paulist Press, 1980.

──── *The Practical and Theological Chapters.* Trans. J. McGuckin. Kalamazoo: Cistercian Publications, 1982.

Modern Authors

BOOSALIS, HARRY. *Knowledge of God*. South Canaan: St. Tikhon's Seminary Press, 2009.

———— *Orthodox Spiritual Life*. South Canaan: St. Tikhon's Seminary Press, 1999.

CHRYSSAVGIS, JOHN. *In the Heart of the Desert*. Bloomington: World Wisdom, 2003.

———— *The Way of the Fathers*. Thessaloniki: Patriarchal Institute for Patristic Studies, 1998.

FLOROVSKY, GEORGES. *Aspects of Church History*. Vaduz: Buchervert., 1987.

———— *Bible, Church and Tradition: An Eastern Orthodox View*. Vaduz: Buchervert., 1987.

———— *Creation and Redemption*. Belmont: Nordland Publishing, 1976.

———— *The Byzantine Fathers of the Sixth to Eighth Centuries*. Vaduz: Buchervert., 1987.

———— *The Ways of Russian Theology*, vols. 1 and 2, Belmont: Nordland Publishing, 1979 and 1987.

GEANAKOPLOS, DENO. *Byzantium*. Chicago: University of Chicago Press, 1984.

HIEROTHEOS, METROPOLITAN. *Orthodox Psychotherapy*. Trans. E. Williams. Levadia: Birth of the Theotokos Monastery, 1994.

———— *The Feasts of the Lord.* Trans. E. Williams. Levadia: Birth of the Theotokos Monastery, 2003.

———— *The Illness and Cure of the Soul in the Orthodox Tradition.* Trans. E. Mavromichali. Levadia: Birth of the Theotokos Monastery, 1993.

———— *The Mind of the Orthodox Church.* Trans. E. Williams. Levadia: Birth of the Theotokos Monastery, 1998.

KESELOPOULOS, ANESTIS. *Passions and Virtues.* Trans. Hieromonk Alexios (Trader) and H. Boosalis. South Canaan: St. Tikhon's Seminary Press, 2004.

LOSSKY, VLADIMIR. *In the Image and Likeness of God.* Crestwood: St. Vladimir's Seminary Press, 1985.

———— *The Mystical Theology of the Eastern Church.* Crestwood: St. Vladimir's Seminary Press, 1976.

MANTZARIDIS, GEORGIOS. *Orthodox Spiritual Life.* Trans. K. Schram. Brookline: Holy Cross Press, 1994.

———— *The Deification of Man.* Trans. L. Sherrard. Crestwood: St. Vladimir's Seminary Press, 1984.

Bibliography 137

MATSOUKAS, NIKOS. *Δογματική καὶ Συμβολικὴ Θεολογία*, vol. 2. Thessaloniki: Pournaras, 1992.

MEYENDORFF, JOHN. *Byzantine Theology*. New York: Fordham University, 1974.

────── *The Byzantine Legacy in the Orthodox Church*. Crestwood: St. Vladimir's Seminary Press, 1982.

OUSPENSKY, LEONID. *Theology of the Icon*, vol. 1. Crestwood: St. Vladimir's Seminary Press, 1992.

POPOVICH, JUSTIN. *Orthodox Faith and Life in Christ*. Trans. A. Gerostergios. Belmont: Institute for Byzantine and Modern Greek Studies, 1994.

ROMANIDES, JOHN. *Δογματικὴ καὶ Συμβολικὴ Θεολογία τῆς Ὀρθοδόξου Καθολικῆς Ἐκκλησίας*, vol. 1, Thessaloniki: Pournaras, 2004.

SCHMEMANN, ALEXANDER. *Of Water and the Spirit*. Crestwood: St. Vladimir's Seminary Press, 1974.

SOPHRONY, ARCHIMANDRITE. *On Prayer*. Trans. R. Edmonds. Essex: Stavropegic Monastery of St. John the Baptist, 1996.

────── *Saint Silouan the Athonite*. Trans. R. Edmonds. Essex: Stavropegic Monastery of St. John the Baptist, 1991.

―――― *We Shall See Him as He Is*. Trans. R. Edmonds. Essex: Stavropegic Monastery of St. John the Baptist, 1988.

―――― *Words of Life*. Trans. Sr. Magdalen. Essex: Stavropegic Monastery of St. John the Baptist, 1996.

STANILOAE, DUMITRU. *The Experience of God*. Trans. I. Ionita and R. Barringer. Brookline: Holy Cross Press, 1994.

―――― *Orthodox Spirituality*. Trans. Archim. Jerome (Newville) and O. Kloos. South Canaan: St. Tikhon's Seminary Press, 2003.

VASILEIOS, ARCHIMANDRITE. *Hymn of Entry*. Trans. E. Brière (Theokritoff). Crestwood: St. Vladimir's Seminary Press, 1984.

YANNARAS, CHRISTOS. *Orthodoxy and the West*. Trans. P. Chamberas and N. Russell. Brookline: Holy Cross Press, 2006.